HYPERDREAM

HYPERDREAM

BY HÉLÈNE CIXOUS

TRANSLATED BY BEVERLEY BIE BRAHIC

polity

Polity Press
65 Bridge Street
Cambridge CB2 1UR, UK

Polity Press
350 Main Street
Malden, MA 02148, USA

ISBN-13: 978-0-7456-4299-4
ISBN-13: 978-0-7456-4300-7(pb)

A catalogue record for this book is available from the British Library.

Typeset in 10.75 on 14 pt Adobe Janson by
Servis Filmsetting Ltd, Stockport, Cheshire
Printed and bound in Great Britain by MPG Books Ltd, Bodmin, Cornwall

For further information on Polity, visit our website: www.polity.co.uk

Ouvrage publié avec le concours du Ministère français de la Culture –
Centre national du livre

Published with the assistance of the French Ministry of Culture –
National Centre for the Book

CONTENTS

Author's Foreword

Intus et in cute

I was anointing my mother. "I am skinning Mummy" I tell myself, doing her skin. It was a little before the end, *tu es le temps*, you are time, killing time, I was thinking, the time of before the end. I was now living in the time before the death of my mother, I watched my mother rise and set day after day on my horizon, overcome with admiration I was living in anguish.

Lately – these last times – I tell myself, I've not stopped feeling everything has changed, all the things that I call "everything" confusedly, have begun to happen completely differently from before the Events. Suddenly I come under the regime of the "last times," I mean the ultimate, the last last, those that are coming up, but which at the same time are in collusion with "lately": the times which have just happened. Some go off into the past, others go off into the future. The difference between the ultimate last times and the lately-last-times is that the latter have a date, whereas the ultimate, no.

The ultimates – the last lasts – I'm in them, I know this now without knowing it except in every pore of my being. These times are divided into two stretches of time, shifting, unstable, like two transparent continents that in turn meet mingle, mix, separate. There's the time before the interruption of my mother. There's the time after the interruption of my friend. Henceforth I am paradoxical. I am before after and after after I am late and I am early I am alreadyafter *déjaprès* and already-before *déjavant* I am tossed into rings within rings, encircled, distanced.

You can always lose more I thought, I twined my thought around this thought, I was anointing my mother with circular gestures, pressing rapidly lightly precisely, no longer shying at the blisters and craters that at the start of the previous year had intimidated me, darting wide cyclopean glances at me whenever I tried to get close to them, my fingers smeared with cream, I didn't dare tell my mother then, last year, that morning and evening I fought with myself, between my powers of reason and my instinct wild with repulsion, it was the idea, an illusion, that the round crevasses edged with a piping of charred skin were looking at me, next thing I knew I'd be putting a finger in their eye, *you can always lose more*, I told myself, absorbed in the meticulous work of encircling and anointing the sores whose constant presence in the end tames the vibrations of mind and soul – and vice versa tames the ulcers and the sores, which let themselves be coated with animal docility. "*I go on living*" I told myself, thought marvelously bitter, bitterly marveling, "*I went on living, therefore losing*," I was thinking, "*it's without end*," if I set this phrase, I was thinking, carefully anointing the back of my mother Eve always beginning with her right shoulder, if I set this phrase devoid of breath and intonation down on a sheet of paper it would have the face of a mask, it would be equivocal, it would be chilling, with the strengthless chill of uncertainty, besides

I myself, on my knees in front of my mother standing, back to the light which enters through the window, I find it strange and sad and saddening, this phrase which comes to me from the far-off bottom of my whole history and at the same time from what is right under my eyes, beneath my nose, my mother's skin upon which I spread, beginning with the upper part of her body and the dorsal face, always in small but regular amounts the contents of a tube of pomade then a second. It crosses my mind that the skin of my mother standing in front of me this July morning in which we go on living, in which, that is, life continues to weave its fabrics within the framework of the body of my mother and within the framework of my body – that my mother's skin, dated, would be the most faithful canvas, or mirror or painting of my most basic, dated state of mind and soul, or of what one calls life, or maybe time's horizon-line on which are painted or deposited the physical effects of what we happen to live. Of what happens to us, living.

I go on living therefore losing, I tell myself, "attacking" as they say, attacking myself, taking myself by the scruff of the neck of my resistances in order to see to the biggest and most recent of the ulcerations, the gutted boil on the underside of her left arm.

This takes us, as they say, most of an hour, this anointing, no rushing it, one's touch must be delicate in order to be precise and painless, moderate therefore. During this hour we don't talk much. A small mass you might say. I don't say this to my mother. Mass is not kosher. You could say a touch of witchcraft.

"I go on living" thinks my mother's body.

– Since they tell me "that's how it is, it doesn't get better" I put up with it, says my mother. – You don't get better from living, I was thinking but I don't say this.

– Turn a little, I say.

In the end death will win. Until the end one doesn't know who wins.

I'll be this skin tomorrow

I anoint my old helmet-maker *ma vieille heaulmière* I confess myself

I'll be this skin tomorrow

And as I anoint her I cultivate time with both hands, one on top of the other hers yours mine ours, I spread them, I browse and I ruminate the future. I study: the way death lets us feel its delicate, intricate bites. How it is already here a little, nibbling. Its inroads. How life gives them back. How it gets its strength and body back by stirring up, citing, resuscitating along the paths of dreams.

And it is during these times, when *all is lost* that I finally come up with the answer to death, the road to happiness *through* pain: this is something-other-than a dream, this is the hyperdream.

I

BEFORE THE END

It was before the end, *tu es le temps*, you are time, killing time, I thought, the time of before the end. Never before had I seen such finished splendor. Suddenly I was warned that I was approaching the point, I saw I could see life glow. It was everywhere. Its dying embers flickered, especially in the leaves and the air. And also in my mother's wide eyes her age makes increasingly prominent You are time I tell her. It was wearing away at my all.

Thursday was the first day of the month of death of my dead my father the dead, my number one dead my first death the fiftieth first day, how fresh this death this dead I was thinking, this death that does not get any older,

I was now living in the time before the death of my mother, I watched my mother rise and set day after day on my horizon, overcome with admiration I was living in anguish, I don't deny occasional moments of exasperation when, at one of those horrible break-of-dawn breakfasts, a fit of having her way suddenly throws the beautiful regularity of her cosmic wheel off balance, it's always to do with the bread, the theme of the bad bread, "I don't like this bread" my mother rasps, meaning: I don't like you I don't like this day I'm tired of this family I don't care for the universe, I bring her, to be sure, a different kind of bread she likes no better, then another, then a sixth, and as I translate her kicks at bread after bread as exactly as I can, I feel fury well up, we are possessed she and I by a pair of demons invisible but tangible who come to blows over the bad bread, fists are flying, we come to two extremes, rage and the grotesque, war quickly breaks out, in this advent of a crimson blackness

if suddenly later, she were no longer here, says my thought choking on the one hand with irritation on the other with fear, were I to lose her right after the blast of this wretched cyclone, at this thought a second storm comes along to coil its atrocious thunderhead up into the Big Temper Tantrum of the Bread, I thought I heard the savage yells of the Worst Thing That Can Happen, one can lose beyond loss, no one is capable of imagining the Worst, one can absolutely not imagine the Worst, one can only say the word Worst – *le Pire*, in French – which is the charred and still crackling remains of the word Prayer – *Prière* – but as the kingdom of the Worst is for after and we dwell in that of its Coming we can't conjure it up, we are only wracked in our bodies, in our bellies, in our hearts by absolutely unbearable spasms. We can't live with it, we want to run away but we can only hop around the table on our left leg because the right is paralyzed.

Later on we try to forget, we burrow into the ground we dig a little time, we wash our hands we forget.

At the same time we remember, but the memory remains in the garden, it goes about its business, it sniffs the stopped-up holes.

That's not how I wanted to begin, I'd just tackled the first page when the racket broke out.

Let me start again. The page would have begun thus: "I can't deny it, I could no longer stop thinking about time, about time and times, I could not, in other words, stop thinking as a worm tries to think sky, clouds, creeping and crawling without ever getting close to a beginning of a slight rise from which to at least catch a glimpse of the sky, and yet I sensed that my whole being, twisted clenched, fired with the urgency of thinking, thought only of turning whatever it is in the act of thinking that takes the place of eyes towards this thing, this subject, this infinite middle ground that we must have good reasons to call *temps* in French, I crepthought in French and in snatches, through rips in curtains through doors left ajar, I knew nothing I saw nothing but I felt strongly, I was led by the name of Time, by the names of time that came and introduced themselves, there are lots of them, it was a necessity, a duty, I wanted I had to understand what I was living on, why and how I was living now that what seemed to me to be "the last times" seemed to have begun.

Lately – these last times – I tell myself I've not stopped feeling everything has changed, all the things that I call "everything" confusedly, have begun to happen completely differently from before the Events that I now see as the causes of a radical change, that is of change at the very root of my being. These last three years I've discovered every day differently and more clearly, day after day, more and more, in the wake of the Diseases that struck two of my nearest and dearest, transformational phenomena of all and everything, and all parts of Everything, have taken place, of which I have gradually grown aware.

Suddenly, but at the time I took no note of this, I come under the regime of the "last times" I mean the ultimate, the last last, those that are coming up, but which at the same time are in collusion with "lately": the times which have just happened. Some go off into the past, others go off into the future.

The difference between the ultimate last times and the lately-last times is that the latter have a date, whereas the ultimate, no.

The ultimates – the last lasts – I'm in them. I know this now without knowing it except in every pore of my being. These times are divided into two stretches of time, shifting, unstable, like two transparent continents that in turn meet mingle, mix, separate, the way our two towers make a single two-souled one in our body. There's the time before the interruption of my mother. There's the time after the interruption of my friend. Henceforth I am paradoxical. This is a very difficult state. I am before after and after after I am late and I am early I am alreadyafter and alreadybefore I am tossed into rings within rings, encircled, distanced, brutally-lengthily, and all this only happens to my body in French, never have my body and I been so much spoken French, "the last times" are times that expose the soul in French, in the English language of my beloved, when there is an upheaval it's *the end*, *The End of the*

World or, as in his metaphysical poem, *The And of the World*. *The End*, *La Fin*, there's another word to drop like a block of ice on a rock, another frightening and empowering word. One ought to break with this word, one ought to punch it in the face, crack open its syllable, drag out of the rubble its secret homonym.

I don't say "death." 1) Death only happened to my father for me. 2) I don't say death. 3) This special word is not the question. After decades of studies and years of analyses of experiments this much I can assert.

This wall word is not the question.

The interruption only interrupts the uninterrupted. It's breathing. About this mystery we always agree, my friend and I. The interruption lets the uninterrupted rest for a moment and lets the interrupted catch his breath.

However the Ultimate, the Last Last Interruption involves innumerable internal modifications. Everything changes, All At Once. In a flash it's as if you were born flung into dark, restless space utterly foreign to the Last Times. No idea where you are naturally, you are shipwrecked, you have only the word *shipwreck* as lantern and explanation, for the rest you're in the dark. All is lost. This lostness – a state you knew nothing about. You are adult and biped but the species is unknown. That's what happened to me. You know nothing about being. Or saying. You don't know. We don't remember this world at all. The world we remember, where we were just last evening has become so far away suddenly you might think you'd dreamed it. It is disqualified. The horror of being zero and without memory without a hint of a link to the being one was and all one feels is that everything I feel has never before happened to me. The moods especially, which are like strangers in my cell who I don't understand what they want – a cargo-load of them clamoring for air, space, as if the cell had the keys. If only I could put a name to one of these slimy bit-parts, if I had an *I* to say, or if I could strike a bargain with one of these creatures, the way people trapped on a train they've boarded by mistake do with the ticket collector. But no ticket collector in sight. Luckily, for I have nothing to show for myself. I feel the consistence and use of a fake. Not my fault all the same. Or rather yes. Poor headless people that I am.

You are no longer anything you know anything about. All you have is Hunger, a Hungering, an unknown Hungering that squeezes, barks orders, pushes and shoves *Faim Fin*: Hunger-End. You don't know how to do anything here, except receive an order in the heart but the body cannot translate. Walk, sure, but how? Go, do, advance, approach, enter? Don't know can't mustn't. Have to. It's

the Interruption that paralyzes me – and whose spell I must break by an act of will I concoct in my head. Think, want, budge in my head. Have to find the exit to can.

Three years I've been battling Paralysis every other day. Always the right leg. Help me I say to my beloved, give me a hand. Always the right leg, as soon as I need to walk, the leg stops, stiffens, sinks into the ground. Pulling it out is torture. I move painfully, slowly. I lean on you. Huge the task, the whole world needs to be invented. I don't lose courage, but time, time and the pain.

Thursday it nearly worked, it was the first day of the month of the death of my father the dead, you were with me, together the two of us, we were about to begin the world over again, it was the Globe Project. Your presence, your warmth, your bulk, our closeness our understanding, our way of being coupled, the way we moved, the accord, the alliance of our bodies as we moved along the Edge: proof, plain, mythical. They'd asked me to create the opera of the creation. I was ready. Off in the distance the conductor nods. The two of us together on the Edge. I took my first steps. No paralysis. I invoked the spaces, I raised a few winds. Methought I conducted the bowels of the air. I raised my arms. I listened. I noticed, at the door to the Globe, that so far I hadn't said anything, merely let them listen to the sounds of the world; I had to begin, probably, utter a word or two, I tell myself, address the invisible peoples, greet those who wait their turn, hidden, I uttered: Friend! Or Friends! But this broke the majesty of the silence.

I almost. I almost made it. A little more and I had grace and all.

Every day I hope the next day to be called upon by the authorities to create the opera of the creation. I wait. You can see the mistake: I should not have thought. To want to do well, what presumption!

You can't anticipate. Wait, obey, let it come. Don't take yourself for more alive, nor more capable than those on the other side. That's the secret. Here we don't do what we want. We only do what is wanted. I manage to say we, we rather than I, it's more prudent.

We don't expect the aid of a waking for this is not a dream. Here is the time of the last times the ones that will happen only once

You can always lose more I thought, I twined my thought around this thought, I was anointing my mother with circular gestures, pressing rapidly lightly precisely, no longer shying at the blisters and craters that at the start of the previous year had intimidated me, darting wide cyclopean glances at me whenever I tried to get close to them, my fingers smeared with cream, I didn't dare tell my mother then, last year, that morning and evening I did battle with myself, between my powers of reason and my instinct wild with repulsion, it was the idea, an illusion, that the round crevasses edged with a piping of charred skin were looking at me, next thing I knew I'd be putting a finger in their eye, *you can always lose more*, I told myself, absorbed in the meticulous work of encircling and anointing the sores, whose constant presence in the end tames the vibrations of mind and soul – and vice versa tames the ulcers and sores, which let themselves be coated with animal docility. "*I go on living*" I told myself, thought marvelously bitter, bitterly marveling, I went on living, *therefore losing*, I was thinking carefully anointing the back of Eve my mother, beginning always with the right shoulder, if I set this phrase devoid of breath and intonation down on a sheet of paper it would have the face of a mask, it would be equivocal, it would be chilling, with the strengthless chill of uncertainty, besides I myself, on my knees in front of my mother standing, back to the light which enters through the window, I find it strange and sad and saddening, this phrase which comes to me from the far-off bottom of my whole history and at the same time from what is right under my eyes, beneath my nose, my mother's skin upon which I spread, beginning with the upper part of her body and the dorsal face, always in small but regular amounts the contents of a tube of pomade then a second. It crosses my mind that the skin of my mother standing in front of me this July morning in which we go on living, in which, that is, life continues to weave its fabrics within the framework of the body of my mother and within the framework of my body, without me for my part having asked for anything, though on my mother's behalf the half that comes down to me, I am forever begging for this and that – that my mother's skin, dated, would be the most faithful canvas, or mirror, or painting of my most basic, dated state of mind and soul, or of what one calls life, this moment of my history, the fifth season, or maybe time's horizon-line on which are painted or deposited the physical effects of what we happen to live. Of what happens to us, living.

I go on living therefore losing, I tell myself, "attacking" as they say, attacking myself, taking myself by the scruff of the neck of my resistances in order to see to the biggest and most recent of the ulcerations, the gutted boil on the underside of her left arm, four centimeters in diameter, queen of the abscessed eyes, corneas with charred lids, a little cadaverized jellyfish, a medusa I was able to look at yesterday for the first time without batting an eyelash. As if after a number of confrontations and flights my soul and it, worn out, had arrived at the peace of mutual surrender: I had shrunk it to its envelope. Now it slips away without resisting and I feel, as I touch what remains with my rubber-capped index, the age-old vanquisher's sentiment of love and pity for the wild thing. Between the burst queen and my index without hostility the slightest tremor of an expiration. The word? Term. The crevasse and I touch at that which offers no grip to any kind of touch: terminal.

"I am going on living that's what I find to think about," I thought, now squatting behind my mother, facing the back of her that I was painting and that was painting me painting what lies in store for me, and I *saw* all the details of this painting that normally we only represent to ourselves in the abstract.

This takes us, as they say, most of an hour, this anointing, no rushing it, one's touch must be delicate in order to be precise and painless, moderate therefore. During this hour we don't talk much. Nothing forbids talking. Except respect for the action being accomplished. A small mass you might say. I don't say this to my mother. Mass is not kosher. You could say a touch of witchcraft

It is a kind of licking. We might be nit-picking. I monkey-groom my mother. It's an occupation.

"I go on living" my mother's body thinks

– Since they tell me 'that's how it is, you don't get better" I put up with it, says my mother.

You don't get better from living, I was thinking but I don't say this.

– Turn a little, I say.

My mother takes a little sideways step. An old little step. Not until she takes the little step does the "old age" theme suddenly clamber into the picture. Not that she's not spry. It's her self-confidence that's diminishing. Confidence is lacking, therefore my mother wobbles at the least awkwardness. I see the thought "uh oh what if I fall" slap a grey shadow on her legs and ankles. She freezes. She recovers her poise, she recovers her eternity.

We don't speak, we ruminate the rite, I don't think, I celebrate methodically, thoughts enter through my hands, through cracks in my breast, gushes of tears, on the inside, marks of spears, slowness application lightning.

Sentences settle, the creature mad for sentences within me opens his or her mouth and bites down on the living, palpitating, oh-so-desirable wee beastie, phrase, phrase, don't run away. I need to keep it alive without swallowing it until the anointing is done. Right away I'll throw it on paper, I'll bed it, I'll fix it, pin it down. Don't let me lose it, I was thinking, saliva purls in my throat, but I am my mother's and only my mother's during this scene and my mother all submission to the anointing

What if we were to talk? Impossible, it doesn't happen. Not-talk during the small mass is part of the mass. We are absorbed. Drunk. We drink. We absorb.

– I wonder if there isn't a cure, in time people come up with things, says my mother, in time, I once knew a bonesetter but he must be dead by now, says humble mother. She says that to lessen my pain, the pain she believes I have, in time, I tell myself, in a few years, a hundred years pretty soon, people go on inventing, the bonesetter too is a gift she doesn't believe in him but there's this word bonesetter, bonesetter, she says, at my age I still have all my words. "He must be dead by now" my mother says. I take this sentence I turn it over, I knead it, I nibble at it. The day of the bonesetter is dead but my mother lives on. There's no cure. She makes do with what you don't get better from. Me too, I make do, I anoint what cannot be fixed

During the mass life goes on in this way: 1) splutter of a motorbike, ancient snore that proclaims: mail. Forty years ago as today, the fateful snore: postman innocent bringer of the verdict. The verdict announced down there, at the foot of the garden behind the forest. Maybe I'm already dead maybe you killed me. I'll find out later. Or resuscitated. Blessed be the dread letterbox. I anoint. I'm all ears. I enjoy. 2) The trees live. The clothes live. My mother stands naked in my study. We are at work. 3) Aletheia enters, back arched, rapid, punctual, squeezes under the couch, expression austere. This signifies: I've got one. To each her sentence. Hers – could it be a cricket? lizard? mouse? I say nothing to my mother. Secrets are secrets.

– Turn a little, I say.

The phrase revolves. Now I see it in profile: "I continue living," I tell myself, I tell myself this phrase and not "I am living." You can't say this phrase without its silent shadow resonating, its opposite invisible twin. I continue: twin: I don't interrupt. I continue instead of interrupting. Saying that, I tell myself, I interrupt a little, I pull towards living, I hold living in my mouth, my expression austere I feel its extreme fragility, its stubbornness a match for its discouragement.

– If you say that, it's because it's in question. It's a way of warding off the contrary, my daughter says. That is, death.

– It's a way to attract the contrary I say, to have the taste of life's dying between your teeth, on the tip of your tongue, the taste of death in life.

I anoint. J'unction. The left arm is a mess. Seat of the rudest combat. It's the earth's west side, which is right now fire and blood. Here a defense there attack. Maneuvers you see with the naked eye. Battalions of murderous cells, blood-soaked trenches.

– It's a deletion of death. It is therefore a barred reconnaissance, barred but recognizable.

In the end death will win. Until the end one doesn't know who wins. As I coat, from time to time the little being under the divan cries out. Job's cry when he gets to the Ear: the indefinite howl of a cricket that is perhaps a mouse. My fate played out under the bed, me unable to do anything about it.

On my knees behind my mother I work. I didn't ask for this, I've become the painter of what in truth escapes me. I continue to live on the back of my mother. Such will have been my mysterious law, forever incomprehensible. That I continue to live at her expense has acquired considerable meaning lately. I only glimpsed the complexity of my law in the days that followed the diagnosis, three years ago now and, to be more precise, from the day I entered the time of the daily ointment although on the first day I probably thought nothing at all, mobilized as I was by the mechanical and material apprenticeship of the execution, the logistics, beginning with the calculation of the quantities, for it is necessary to distribute evenly over the entire surface of the body

the contents of two tiny tubes of cream which seem at first glance insufficient to coat a single limb.

Nonetheless on the first day of the application, the features of the as-yet-unthought figure came together and all that was missing was time for the mind to wake up and receive the message formed in the frame. It takes time to get around to reading. You can walk past the signs a thousand times without seeing there is book. Afterwards read does not signify having understood, naturally.

I see myself on my knees before my mother's upright body, then kneeling, the way I see it her body is divided into several bodies and states of bodies, according to the path my hands take for one and for another my thoughts, my hands in one order and my thoughts coming and going from my mother's body to all the human states of which the body is the character, states, scenes, war, peace, anguish. I always begin by the back of the right shoulder, not at all therefore as if I were writing from left to right on my sheet of paper, but on the sheet of my mother, erasing as I go, then I descend in the same manner down the back to the buttocks, including Eve's flanks in this first body, the south. Then I do the north face from the neck to the tops of the thighs and this is the second body. Next we do the legs down to the feet. The feet I leave to her. This is the third body. Let's add the skin, a world in itself, with its exceedingly varied formations of creases, pleats, bosses, tucks.

Without this Malady, which is not a malady, I shouldn't find myself today and every day to come in reality *face to life*, I mean in front of or behind the back of my mother, forced naturally to see in front of me everything that would otherwise have remained locked up in my heart of hearts, the laws and figures of my destiny as human being, common mortal, and unique singular specimen, arising from a conjunction of events and accounts of events in large part yet to be discovered.

But this illness (which is however not a real illness, but a complex and exceedingly rare natural phenomenon) would all by itself probably not have struck my mind, as opposed to my heart or habits, with such vivacity had it not declared itself at almost exactly the same time as the illness of my friend, the one fast upon the heels of the other a week apart, in the space of a week two maladies that strike two of the five or six people closest to me, it's as if they'd botched beheading me, two attempts and in vain, half-severed head dangling I live I have no choice.

If my friend's illness (which is not however just an illness but above all a destiny and not just a personal and worldwide tragedy, but an unbearably pure blow of fate, one of those sorts of fates whose features are outlined in Antiquity with proportions details circumstances so absolutely implacable you know beyond a doubt they belong to the mythical imagination, hence it is impossible that they should ever in reality occur, nevertheless precisely because such an event is impossible it happens to occur) had been diagnosed a week after my mother's illness, during the week which in that case would have followed upon the diagnosis, wrong what's more, initially, and which announced a rapid, fatal outcome, I would have entered the cage full of savage phantasms that is abruptly attributed to us under such circumstances, but not all by myself, not without having telephoned my friend, counting of course on his viaticum, not without leaning on my beloved albeit discreetly as ever so as not to inflict on him too heavy a penalty

But what took place was the opposite. First I received my friend's Malady and hadn't yet embraced it when I received my mother's Malady, for some time I could not complain to one of the other, I no longer knew whom to think of first, I thought of him of her of me, I was ravaged by the flame of a crazy logic, I thought of him thus of her thus of me, then I thought of him not thus of her thus of me half me then of her thus of me half him then of Nothing, a freezing endless Nothing a bottomless and slow and desert and glacial well, I no longer knew how to think, I gave up thinking. Alone in the cage with the lion and the python, we devoured one another, not told my friend not told my love. Not told my mother, lied the fatal Illness (which is not in truth exactly fatal only announcement of death, wake-up, tick-tock all over the body skin watch) not told Mummy the utterly beyond words, what's on your body there, that's the letter, not a word at least during the first days of the final last times, a false diagnosis passing for true for eight days roaming the corridor of the mother, one doctor, two doctors, three doctors, at the fifth the outcome was not fatally rapid but merely fatal according to whether it was rapid or slow, it was the Malady of the final last times, the bizarre angel of the last act, the one who comes to give you time to think about that about which we know not whether to make ourselves think or not think, "the end" en route, that about which we don't for years especially the last ones, it all depends, stop thinking and sometimes during all the years from the age of reason on, which as it transpires is the reasonable slope of dementia, taking each new year for the last one and making three hundred and some attempts a year to stage the final last act with a wealth of imaginary versions.

(I myself have just conjured up our death, which I do not know yet, that of my beloved and me, this took place yesterday, in Japan, in Tokyo, the death had happened just a few days earlier who'd have thought such a thing, and here we are in a foreign but most welcoming land, lodged in a hotelpital, fêted, garlanded with flowers like newborns burbling their first encounters with a world of which we know nothing. So much goodwill. Of course we will no longer be able make love, I didn't complain. I've always known one can make love in other ways without making love. But you, you apologized a little, this is because you're a man, and delicate.)

We don't stop killing ourselves. We die one another here and there my beloved and I, it's an obsession, it's an exorcism, it's a feint, what we are feigning I have no idea is it a sin a maneuver a vaccination the taming of a python the fixing-up of the cage, it's an inclination, we don't stop rubbing up against our towers touching our lips to them, clearly this is like worshiping the Torah, eroticism to the nth degree lips on the sacred scroll, the innocent handle of the book, the saint, the simpleton, we know all about it, we'd always thought it, we'd also always feared for our towers, such striking clarity, and naked, but what terror when the real planes really crashed into them, a black terror that bit into our hearts, so this in reality can happen, in reality there was a tomb on one of our bodies, this was a fact, and no waking, we'd awakened assassinated. This is an alert. Worse – what the alert utters it prophesies. No escape. Each time I've gone to Montaigne since the massacre of our *Twins*, our beloved totems erect frail black funeral tapers planted in the synagogue of my heart, I make my way impurely, heart fretful, every superstition cajoled and enlisted, I myself jail and the jailed, I go wounded, bite-marked, distrustful, prepared for the worst instead of racing not touching the earth towards the adorable, dearly beloved originary Tower, mother Tower fiancée, ready to accuse it, alas, I go there more and more often, it's obsessive, in the old days I would come here occasionally, deliberately, I used to enjoy conjuring it up, magnifying it in my mind, making a tale of it, I saw it shimmer in my thoughts, I didn't go, this was the sign that it was eternal, that it would be there forever, I made it wait, desire, I pretended to forget what delight I had, the willful make-believe unfaithfulness of faithful lovers, I had all the attributes of ownership. As long as our two towers were alive I don't seem to know how achingly I love it. Since their death, all the suffering, all the scare-baby games – which I now see we'd always lodged in New York, our store of poisons entrusted to the *Twins*, counting of course on the jumbo apparatus of the American passions, in sum the whole anxious and maleficent game – of our lives, our primitive beliefs, our frissons, the deadly Greek- and Bible-inspired phantasms, all that ghastly archivery we'd intuitively conserved in our Manhattan towers – hence unconsciously used as the colossal envelopes of all ideas of catastrophe, coffins costumed as the temples of our death wishes –

this store of our unknown misfortunes has been transferred to our good tower of Montaigne, I note, chagrined. I can't stop wanting to go there, going to Montaigne has become a nervous tick, a reason to awake with a jerk, I've been stung, the idea that if I don't go tomorrow it will vanish therefore us along with it I reject, feebly, I can't all the same spend my life dashing off to Montaigne, beside there are rites, I need my brother first of all, my love next, our tower expects certain ceremonies, and my brother, my brother the attendant of our meticulous weddings, my brother is wearing out, how can I continue using him to run off to Montaigne, I fret, I resign myself to what is,

if the Tower our mother our body our sex burned down tonight – the hypothesis cannot be rejected, the whole castle has already burned down except for the Tower, and how to think this extraordinary event: the-whole-castle-burned-except-the-Tower, how to make sense of it? Does this mean the castle paid for the Tower? Or that the Tower's turn will come, since what else remains to burn? How what's more to explain that such a tower, such a perfect gem of human grandeur not be condemned and executed in these days of perverse criminality? For sure it's a target, plans are afoot. She loses nothing by waiting. She is there, round, delicious, appetizing, eternal, pregnant with genius and with books and she is not there. One gulp of the plane. We are already killed. Read all about it in tomorrow's paper –

if the Tower has burned, we are already dead and tomorrow we shall die of it

If the Tower has not yet burned, it will burn in a day or two. This hypothesis sends me scurrying off towards our incarnation. So what if this is folly. Who can define the status and value of a presentiment? Rush right over won't save it tomorrow, I know that. What gets me onto the road is the disgraceful and cruel law of farewell. I want to see her. I won't tell a soul, not even my beloved, not even myself, the vague intentional silhouette I believe I glimpse grazing the walls of my inner cinema. All is shadow –

I acknowledge the feverishness of my new mental illness. I am capable of not yielding to my own blackmail, I have the strength. But say the tower burns this week, I'd never forgive myself. *You can go on losing after loss*. I recognize the theme of my chief anguish: the theme of the last hour. The Pain greater than pain is not to have the right and the opportunity of the actual last hour I tell myself. In the place of the last hour I make a few pragmatic concessions: I locate it in the general vicinity of the loss, in the few hours that accompany it to the grave, it is a variable measure of time. I remain modest in my precautions. I always "say" adieu to someone dear to me when the circumstances include an objective risk, if for instance one or the other of them is taking a plane. However, I do not utter the word "adieu." I have my words and signs. It is essential to have exchanged the invisible ring for all that we call survival, survive, survivor. All these words go on living today in the numerous public, private, secret texts and scrolls my friend devoted to them. When I say invisible ring, this is a metaphor. Each of us substitutes for the ring whatever his or her civilization suggests

Still, I'm not a machine for bidding adieu. Only I make the necessary arrangements, naturally. It's part of my daily routine, like washing my face. Naturally some days have no adieux.

Moreover I plead the appropriateness of my attitude. True, it is a religion. But private, erudite and perfectly well calculated. To be afraid is the condition of loving knowledge. Were I not dying of fear, I'd not know how to exist myself, I wouldn't get the notices of existence, I wouldn't record with delight the minuscule passage off to the right of a blue tit, its wing dipped in gold on the dusk. Were I not dying of sorrow I wouldn't with nostalgia be present at the creation of the world, the squirrel nuptials this morning I wouldn't care. Creatures are born to a backdrop of adieux.

Still were I to end up calling my brother, at this moment of the book that I so ardently desire to start to write, it would be in order to put an obstacle in the way of my desire, to put off what I most desire in the whole world lately, that is to write a book, whatever it may be, for what simmers inside me like the fires of an infection is the too cogently argued fear of being unable to write, and that no book will come along to save me, a too-natural fear which welled up a day or two after my friend's terrestrial interruption or maybe that very day. But to that I can't bear witness for I only took a kind of vague and devastated cognizance of the real effects of the disaster that had put out the eyes of the world and me some time Afterwards but right away I felt the total mutation of Creation into Destruction. Right away I felt that Destruction is an Activity whose terms and bounds none can conceive, that manifests itself in all directions, all institutions, all details. On the one hand the whole world is drained of its blood, and on the other, in a flash a worldwide infestation of the brains and hearts of all those who waited, hunkered down with hopeless patience hence necessarily hidden under dull appearances, hopeless but teeming and chewing their muzzles with resentments, all those who congenitally despaired of the withdrawal of the Supreme Good, all the envious the querulous withdrawn and too time-mummified for one to have counted them before the explosion. I'd never seen anything like it. You haven't got the strength. You are exchanged for a ghost, you wake up in an exylum. Who in the world could raise the slaughtered bull of the world? And the impotence of my ghost, every day growing. The books withdraw as I imagine the soldiers of a lost battle retreat. From this point onwards there's nothing to wage. To book on. Something great and glorious turns gaseous. The Rescue Squad can rescue only those still in a state to be rescued and a little lame. So the books fade away. You can't rescue the Rescuers. In the end I'll call my brother, even before I have finished mulling it over, am I not called? How not respond to the call of our Tower? Mightiest are the calls without voices. It's like when Philia with her dizzying eyes begs for something to eat. No way to pretend I didn't see the voice of her eyes. As if I didn't hear the steady green purity of my cat's hunger. She shows me her limpid face which hunger's authority puts under arrest. I obey. If God had seen Job's eyes. But no. *Dieu n'a pas d'yeux*. God has no eyes. *Il n'y a pas Dieu*. No God. No eyes.

I'll be this skin tomorrow. There's no doubt I like the back best. I stick to the back, it has an ageless delicacy. The skin is of a lightly rose-tinted white with a hint of straw. In the middle of the back, down to the waist, a sprinkling of brighter pink spots marble the epidermis before the skin gets its freedom and fineness back on the buttocks.

The old age is all in the legs. The sags, the ripples, the gullies, the rucks of the integument of the thighs, the swellings, the marks of age's violent blows, the arterial tubing, no doubt about it, this is human old age.

I anoint my old helmet-maker *ma vieille heaulmière* I confess myself

I'll be this skin tomorrow

And as I anoint her I cultivate time with both hands, one on top of the other hers yours mine ours, I spread them, I browse and I ruminate the future, casqued old age, she's in the pink of health

Save for the extraordinary Malady, which however is not a malady pure and simple, but a death notice, a little reminder from the vital administration, a circular sickness or sick circular almost entirely reserved for the very old in the pink of health thus for practically no one. Only those going on a hundred need apply, without this Malady their excellent health might go to their heads, it's a malady for the exceedingly rare skeptic. Hosted by only an infinitesimal proportion of the population naturally it is left out in the cold. Most doctors die without ever having set eyes on it. It is a curiosity for me bordering on horror, this representation I could do without, of the work of the decomposing administration on the body of my mother, I'd rather not know about it,

they ask us for a down-payment, I complain, I refuse, I side with the skin of my mother, aided by my mother's perfect health and her radical powers of resistance to dire images, the inflexibility of her imagination, the rigidity of her reasoning which has always stood like a steel wall before any ravings, especially mine, hallucinations, the undeniable fact of the existence of ghosts, specters, shades she denies without so much as a shade of denial, my mother is a terrestrial fortress, she sees only the describable visible. The invisible, the unpredictable, all that impends and gets ready, behind, under, on the sides, above, allusions, analogies, hints, insinuations, coincidences, symptoms, none of the faceless powers that make my heart beat interest her

her Malady either, even this Malady albeit the last and undeniably monstrous and terrifying, whose description I could read only in English, feeling my soul *cringe* before the harshness and the density of the hyper-threatening and maleficent metaphorical messages, the description existing only in English, in highly specialized scientific journals, so rare is this malady, addressing itself only to one in a million, the almost centenarian in excellent health, a person who, without this malady, might believe themselves closing in on non-mortality, it has no global market value and no interest even for science's peculiar appetite, since it concerns but one in a million and one by definition of very short duration.

When all's said and done I tell myself, dabbing with a kind of acquired boldness at the burst vesicle plump as an oyster under her left arm, this malady speaks directly and indirectly to me as my mother-to-be and guardian of my mother here present, all these withered puckered lips address their recriminations and regrets from pus-filled sinkholes to me, my mother is deaf, she doesn't listen, she has a diminishing inborn strength in the place of all events, lucky and unlucky alike, whence her longevity and consequently this final last malady, reserved for cases like the maternal one. Were I to tell her that her crevasses and her vesicles speak, that indeed all her body openings have always spoken since the night of time, and not just the wounds of princes assassinated in Greek and Shakespearean tragedies, that everything that opens her speaks, even a suitcase, but this I don't say.

I'll be this skin tomorrow, I tell myself.

I am practicing. When we have passed ninety first my beloved then me five years later, in the hypothesis, not to be rejected out of hand, that this malady, exceedingly rare, insofar as it is one reserved for ninety-going-on-a-hundred-year-olds, strikes us you first probably, or both of us together, will I be able to kiss your vesicles or your crevasses? Yes. Will I be able to lick the lips of your wound? Yes. Consider it done.

I stop at pus. I fear you will say no. I fear the shudder. One doesn't know oneself twenty years on. I practice on my mother. Theory, my mother says, is zero. Only practice counts.

A disease for fools. Malady-Comedy: the skin no longer recognizes itself. It attacks itself, feeds on itself; persecutes itself. A mental illness complete with all the tricks of Mental Illness. It has a goal: no matter the cost hold on right to death. You notice that the attacks are programmed according to an incurable strategy, by means of quick shifts. Mobility, virulence, the Malady thinks, not a shadow of doubt. It proceeds via harassment hence diversion and perversion. The Skin is itself both Malady and Patient, you cannot imagine a more disheartening situation.

Skin is everywhere, so is the disease. Best not think about it, for at the thought of the skin being itself a virtual skin you can expect mental blisters to erupt

Any victory on one front signifies prompt reprisal in a free zone. No respite. In general malady and hostage find no issue but fatal. Most of the time, they jump out the window together.

The window solution is so frequent (20% of cases) that some researchers call it the "window stage" and seem to think that the window is felt by the skin to be a giant blister giving rise to an irresistible suicidal itch.

I make joints, I attempt to close, to wall up fissures and cracks, to plaster over her surface, block, meanwhile I confess.

Intus et in cute says Perse says Rousseau, one always confesses inwardly and at the surface of the skin, and vice versa the skin, if observed, brings on the confession. Given the chance. Something about the contemplation of the skin makes us speak. I've noticed this.

It's a close-up, a blow-up of the same minuscule.

No being is as docile as confiding as the skin – countenance of the back, all the more docile and consenting and defenseless as this skin, this back, is the protection-requiring abstract of the person who has always helped and protected me, first my grandmother and then my mother, my mother taking over the place and function of her mother our grandmother.

This back provides food for thought on many levels. Politically, poetically, ecologically, medically, philosophically, thought of the skin. Skin of thought. The most beautiful text of my friend whose every text is beautiful each in a different way, the most beautiful in my opinion I tell myself, because the most cruel – the most flayed, the most stripped, the most hideous to the eyes, the most scabrous, had it not oozed from the lips of the scars of his mother's body, in other words had the skin of his mother not opened those small mouths and let all the wordless pain in the world ooze out, he would not have happened, my friend, to find himself in a state of confession.

We have not yet started to think about the skin I tell myself, this can be explained in part by the rareness of opportunities for a face-to-face with the skin, particularly the skin of a superior venerated and supposedly omnipotent person.

I've got to the shoulder blades in my hour of confession, fully occupied with rumination and reminiscence I see your back through my mother's back I see your back of today, your back of Thursday at my breast. Last Thursday. I hear it, I hear a murmur your skin speaks, a blood thinks, I hear your thought running under the skin I hear your life thinking under the neat eternal spotless silk. I read with my life. I am torn. At the same time I am healed and glued back together again. During this time the world suffers and dies

– Haunted?

– Yes.

– What are you thinking?

– The same thing: During this time we live. We are torn.

– Turn a little, I say to my mother.

You scarcely shift. You are on the left side. The light of Thursday comes in through the window at our back. Always we are back to the light, after love. Always returning to the world you go first I guard you and the light follows. Shadows of your thoughts that I glimpse beneath the skin of your back to which shadows of my thought respond.

– Rippled, I say. I ripple you. I put my lips on you to bring you peace, so that you may be sure of yourself.

– Montaigne, you say. He had more confidence in him, in the beloved, than in himself.

The way my mother allows herself to be looked after. I lift her right arm, push it a notch forward, I dab at the clots. An act of confidence that doesn't know its name. There's no poem no poetry no citation no name. Only the manner. The doing.

How I admire the quiet of the wordless manner. I can't bear it. Her: in her skin. Meanwhile I am in the between-time of time with my love, we think, it makes everything tremble you say, last Thursday. Last Thursday is now in the room in which I anoint Mummy. I cite here the hour pulled out of our history. It is still warm, golden, arranged, complete. Later I shall forget it. I hold onto it by its sentences still, by its fringe, by the tones of its voices

"He had more faith in him than in himself."

I have more faith in you than in myself says your voice

– You are right says my voice

– Especially when you are off in Bordeaux says your voice

Bord d'eau bord dos says the echo *dos do*

Edge of sea edge of back lullaby

I cite our scene in the room where my mother is all confidence in me whom she calls "daughter," "*ma fille*."

– Mummy, say I. – Daughter says she. – You are right, say I. Daughter say I. Mummy, says she.

My mother never asks what I am thinking. She asks what I want to eat *tomorrow.* I wonder where we'll be next year Jerusalem 14. I rummage in my heart a bit, but that starts an insignificant pain, the nibble-nibble of a scarcely formed ghost, only the pain returning floors me. The things one imagines are as nothing at all in comparison to those which recommence, unhappiness, happiness.

I live on the hypothesis that our tower is intact. But it's all a hypothesis. Am I living? or have I turned back? All I can do is call my brother to go the tower. Let's go to the Tower I say, but I don't say let's go *check on* the Tower, I don't want to show the twists and turns of my mind, I disapprove of myself all by myself, the anguish is my business, let's go to the Tower, say I, whenever you like dear says my brother, now that my brother is behind me I can't retreat. I do nothing the easy way. It's the price to pay for the Tower I tell myself. I pay a high price, what else can I do? The Tower is my abscess. It is better thus. All my folly is battened into the strong back of the worshiped cylinder. But to go to the Tower is a detour, a side-trip, dangerous, a trench I dig between my book and me, I see the plan: I dig and I erect and I sacrifice the lamb. Seeing doesn't keep my life from ravaging itself, fastened as it is to a few endangered bodies. But in another way *go to see the Tower* always has a dew effect, every time I go, I see with my own eyes that it exists, the cracks are just the same, she is invincible my brother will say, as if he were talking about my mother, this keeps me going for a while. All the same I cannot *live with* the Tower, of the Tower, on the Tower. Still, something vital attaches me to it as scroll, vase, column countenance of higher alliances. That my compulsion in one way verges on mental illness is a fact largely compensated for in another way by what goes with it, I mean the alliance with my brother. Owing to the tower temptation that has developed and rigidified these past years the brother–sister plot has thickened. My brother has become my brother-who-never-says-no. My mother says why, my brother says yes. Thus at one and the same time I can *check* on the resistance of the Tower and on the resistance of the my-brother-and-I pact to the attacks of time. I make sure of the solidity of the Tower and at the same time of the endurance of the brother–me friendship. My brother has never asked *why* the minute I arrive in the region I call him to go the Tower one of these days. Never made the least commentary. If he has begun to notice that each time I indulge in checking up on the Tower and around it I haven't noticed. While I check he remains three paces behind and munches a sandwich. Perhaps he has noticed nothing at all for I do this fast and discreetly I run down the metonymic chain with all the unerringness of a plumber-mason, I inspect the surroundings, the paths, but above all the body, each fissure is inside me, each round muscle, each crack each sign of wear I make sure the Tower is in good condition overall, all the organs and out-of-the-way corners in which we have deposited a thought, I auscultate them I let the handful of visitors among them my brother, who counts for two and plays straight-guy, go by while I come and go between floors, I sound, I examine, I calm down, but perhaps my brother takes no notice my tour of inspection, thus over the years he has acquired the role of double and shield, I shelter behind his stiff back, I check the donkeys are in their pasture and that the cat is around. I add that I check on my brother also. Inconceivable my brother should fail me.

My brother launches into a repetition of his own, but of another sort. First of all, he keeps it for the itinerary of our outing, it is a hundred-kilometer-long hymn of praise whose intense charm is linked to the names of the places we traverse, which he accompanies with a brief unchanging commentary. I never say to my brother: I've heard that a dozen times before. For the charm is partly due to the absolute exactitude of the verbal reproduction right to the semantic nuances and tones of voice. My brother's chant has a mythic freshness. This gives each expedition the colors of a first time. I've reached the point of expecting and ticking off. Recognize this road? says my brother, Fargue Saint-Hilaire Comarsac interesting town Saint-Pey-d'Armens Saint-Quentin-de-Baron, they do sepulchers, Hollywood-style theme park we treat your dead like VIPs rejected by the population Grézillac Le Moine Pey de Prat, our old friend the Dordogne – we didn't put down roots in Algiers says my brother we were all alone in our solitude, welcome to St Jean City Saint-Jean-de-Blaignac Branne Hôtel de France, Cabara says my brother 120 inhabitants and a crime that splendid Farm where a man killed a man says my brother each year happiness is a mixed blessing and each year a man kills a man, bliss someone is killed Pont de la Donne Pujols Castillon La Bataille where the Battle was won and lost the sky and its cloudy constructions in the water and the acacias on the quay Talbot's sword on the path to the grapevines Lavagnac brought from the South do you know what this street is called Promenade of the Allies, every year men fall and are resuscitated, my brother sings the wars that doze in the stones Mister Talbot sleeps so far from home, the Allies go walking, I see the shades of the defunct sleeping the sleep of death rise up, warrior throngs fallen under the bronze and the helmets under six centuries of memory weapons still drip blood along the Promenade of Oblivion and Memory Cabara says my brother 120 inhabitants, one crime, by dint of making and reciting it this road has become the road of the Allies and the Forgotten. I don't know if we made up the alliance between the road and the Tower my brother and I by digging a tunnel through time or whether it is the road that did this, because of the so rich sentence it traces in space conducting us unawares through the fields of time. You who survive a while you will die and we will live on the villages nod, the public wash-houses, the trees, the dwelling places. Never will one see a cemetery so alive and so cultivated, I was thinking. This is our cemetery without a tomb, I tell myself. Never would I breathe a word of this to my brother. Never what's more have I been able to begin work on piece of literature that wasn't lit up by a Tower. I'd never have written my thesis on Joyce had I not been taken in hand forty years ago by the *Martello Towers*. I live on the hypothesis that our Tower is intact. This is a hypothesis. But what happens if one day I call my brother and he wounds my rite. This is a hypothesis I do not wish to envisage. For my brother and the Tower form an originary ensemble, this took place in the night of time, and since that night and since that time whenever I think Tower I think my brother, and since that time, for thirty years first with my brother then with my love, first with the fraternal exergue then with my beloved, first the preface and no book without preface, as soon as I turn or am turned towards our Tower, I call my brother, and only my brother, these past few years moreover it is my brother, and not I nor my love, who has taken on something of the Tower, it's imperceptible, a dreamy rounding or perhaps a secular density, like a natural persistence, nothing humanly fleshly, and which takes shape within a being by dint of repeating some adventure over and over again. I am wretched. It isn't that I want to go to the Tower. It's that I can't tell the image of the Tower within me that I won't hurry over. The Authority that makes me will agree to some accommodations: as soon as the trip has been decided upon, it's as if I had set out, the actual date is negotiable, I can put it off for a day, if my brother keeps me waiting. If there is some kind of delay, change, this is OK. The Authority has no face that I know of, in place of a face a deadly will. Truly, only a dead person can exercise such absolute authority over a person under him. You don't talk back to the deceased. When all I can do is prepare to call my brother, at this point in the book I so ardently wish to begin to write the presentment of an intention contrary to that which I believe to be my main impulse steals over me, like an inexplicable intruder in a dream: perhaps within me the desire to put off that which I most in the world desire of late keeps watch, I mean, to write a book but a wounded book, a contentious, broken book, a book not pleased to be a book, to be only a book, to be born in the absence of my friend, a book incapable of acting as if the last times were not upon us, but which at the same time cannot act as if it were only a book hence a being unaware of the end, unaware what time it is. The idea of the book, of which I am unable to think without blanching, paces my halls. I should want not to think about it whereas the desire does not go away. I decide to call my brother. "If the Tower is still there" I tell myself. There's the point I'd reached.

– I'm going to call my brother, I tell the back of my mother. My mother says: "You are going to see the donkeys? Do you think they'll recognize you?" For her the donkeys are the Tower. The Tower is just about everything for me. For her the Tower is the oldest beginning of the mental illness she blames me for keeping festering and away from any healing temptation. My mother does battle with the ghost of Montaigne's Tower within me like the symptom of a plague that has received the stamp of my approval, I say *Tour* for Tower, she says *Four* for Oven. She pushes the Tower aside, a windy book mill. She wasn't there when I was nineteen and we met for the first time. I thought Talbot was a literary character, I walked past his meager tomb before which Montaigne, coming along a hundred years after *the battle*, reined in his little horse to think for a moment of death. Its refinements, its wellspring of malignancy. Seeing that Talbot, who judged himself a great captain when he brought the city of Bordeaux under English rule, now lies alone and henceforth under three stones and two foreign pebbles. That we must not judge of our fortunes until after death and the funeral ceremonies. Here lie the dead for whom Montaigne came along too late, I tell myself. On the unvisited mound. Here is where Montaigne took from Talbot who had once taken Bordeaux from him the lesson to die neat and of an ending composed to perfection and to try to bury himself in the lap of his Tower.

We, a family without land, without tombs, I might have thought: I'll end in a book with Mummy beside me. – Too bad I wasn't around when you happened upon this Tower, I was in Algiers and you take a fancy to this matrix of stone. Some people wage a struggle for health, she says, with you it's a sickness.

Everything about the Tower she reviles. In the old days I say there were no donkeys. It doesn't surprise me there are donkeys now. For her the donkeys are metamorphoses. The Tower as a whole for her is the donkey. Everything I believe in – I play the donkey. I always stick to my guns, says she. I'm for health you are for sickness. Your Tower is a sickness. She tacks on: your donkeys, your Tower, your malady. All the possessives are on my side, the side of the possessed. Although it is totally unfair at the moment I am just the victim of the idea of contagion. Everything seems and everything speaks to me everything scolds me and warns: why shouldn't tomorrow be the last day of my Tower, there's no proof, it's when you least expect it that it comes tumbling down that my Tower is struck by the American explosion and the murmur of my own heart, but why shouldn't it be? I say: "My Tower" and fear dazzles me. All the same no other place in the world gives me such a feeling of peace, provides a glimpse of immortality with an address on earth, but only if I can put my hands on it, if I feel it, if I run my fingers over its fissures and inventory them once again, even the fissures cracks moss mold reassure me, I have founded all my will-power and everything I do on its native tenacity: it is as it has always been. However, because of a strange passion, from a distance I lose it to almost the opposite hypothesis: precisely because it is so strong so modest so voluptuous being so well protected from within by the maxims of eternal wisdom that have resisted the wear and tear of the centuries hence the chains of the wars of religion it *would seem* that lightning keeps watch in order to demonstrate the absolute and absolutely arbitrary power of the principle of the destruction of the indestructible. The stronger my Tower the greater the threat of this that and the other. My brother reads the obituaries in the paper me I turn my imagination here, there and elsewhere without cease for I am in risky country. Phantasms eat at my Tower.

When I hear it creak and groan in the depths of night among the smoky curtains, uttering human moans I start up in my bed crying Mummy! Mummy! I'm coming! And under my eyes I see the little old lady wrapped in flames crumple to her foundations. In my opinion one spark and torch is the word. In my mother's opinion the Tower is the sum of everything that is bad for your health, a monument to the book a mill to grind donkeys.

She says the donkeys for the Tower. Me too, whenever I think of my beloved Tower, I think of the two donkeys. The donkeys are us we said as soon as we saw them, from the very first time they appeared to us as our hairy emanations, but I don't say this to just anyone, right away they came to us for we appeared the same to them. Montaigne also recognized himself now as donkey now as his cat now in that little horse with whom he set off against death on fine days. We saw ourselves as Job and Carrot Top. – What are you going to do with your brother in this Tower where you've already been more often than not? Beats me. Something new with the donkeys? What do you know about the donkeys? I say. I know, says my honest mother. I know they are very stupid. – It's in your dictionary? – It's in reality. No budging a donkey. You think they recognize you? If they do it's by mistake. I recall being on a bridge once on my way to Oran. We couldn't get by. The donkey was in the middle, gazing at its mother, like a chunk of wood. No way to budge it. Here I am here I stay. Don't you know donkeys are like that? Well I knew! trumpets my mother. – It reassures me the donkeys stay. – I don't think you can teach a thing to a donkey. I've never been on a donkey, ever. I've never been in the Tower. It seems they're a mixture not a race. It seems to me there are two sorts of donkeys says my honest mother. That of which she is unsure she does not affirm. Some are bigger some are smaller. I need to check my dictionary. She takes her dictionary, the faithful German. *Das Lexikon der Hausfrau. Esel* I'm looking for, she says. It's her book. The useful and the necessary. The housewife's dictionary. *Der Esel ist nicht da* she says. Before there's *Erziehung*. After is *Essig*. *Esel* is not between Education and Vinegar. I don't get it says my mother why it's not in here. She finds *Eselohren*. It's very bad in books to grow *Eselohren*. *Eselhaft* to be stupid as a donkey. Truly they have a poor reputation. I've never been interested in donkeys, stubborn as can be. At the moment I'm reading a novel by Daphne du Maurier. It is very interesting.

I call my brother. It occurs to me maybe I should stay home with my mother. It occurs to me perhaps the donkey is not where I think. The donkey is not in the dictionary. Before there is education after there is vinegar.

My mother writes me a letter. "*My darling daughter, despite my age and the certainty of death in the program I continue to behave as if I were going to be here with you for a long time, you so tender and vulnerable you need an old tower to live so go ahead I regret being unable to keep you company on your little outings I've always been curious about new places but I no longer have the strength and it is perhaps German romanticism that throws the young who no longer include me on the road. Die Wandervögel.*" She leaves the letter on my desk.

I call my brother, tomorrow we aren't going to Montaigne as usual but to the Ocean, which is right next to my mother and quite the contrary from the Tower, after my mother's letter I could absolutely not do otherwise. One must sacrifice a tower to save a Tower I tell myself, but I contrived to suggest to my brother that we take a little trip to the Ocean.

My mother steps modestly out of the bathroom, without so much as a sideways glance, the side where I write with my door open to my mother who makes no effort to be noticed not knowing how, what I write is of no interest to her, nose down, lengthened by the aging of the skin of her face which is growing smaller,

– Shall I do your back? I say.

She doesn't ask: do my back, ever. She thinks neither of asking nor of not asking. Her strength lies in her docility to whatever comes.

Sometimes I am off traveling, I think of her back without me, it makes me ill, she makes me ill, sometimes I forget to do the back, sometimes I remember I have forgotten, sometimes I don't remember, sometimes I don't feel like doing it, I examine this notfeellike, it is made up of boredom, the boredom is caused by the mechanical repetition of gestures over the same surface, this makes doing my mother's back analogous to riding an exercise bike, doing lengths in a pool or any other sport that channels the head's force into the limbs, the legs or the arms, leaving the head empty, given to yellowish boredom. Notfeellike is very strong. Later on, I tell myself, I'll remember these moments of laziness – desire in reverse, negative voluptuousness, luxury – what today bores me, that I want done fast so much so that I coat at top speed teeth clenched – will make me weep. Somewhere I shall put in a book – when perhaps I'll have to struggle to get the same forever lost scene down on paper – when I'll have to summon up all my strength in order to remember a smidgeon of my mother ferociously far-off-and-lit like a Rubens my mother naked in front of me wreathed in tears, I think, this moment of raw beauty, of raw boredom, brought to life by a shameless gesture of flight, spent, squandered, I will envy it, the frame will be the same but hard-edged and all the feelings changed into their opposites, alas how happy I would be I'll think, I think, were I able to do now that it is impossible what I had no wish to do when I had to coat my mother in cortisone ointment, how happy I was when I didn't know it I'll think, at this moment bored stiff I coat for I am mortally asleep like all beings who suffer from Good Health, Good Health is the most insidious of maladies, I tell myself this, in vain, I am alive asleep and although I exhort myself to wake I am as powerless to break the spell as if I wanted to break out of a dream in a dream and I know I shall wake once my mother is dead and therefore myself. Later I'll want to revive this boredom, bring it to life again I tell myself, but it will have perished and the more I want it the more feebly it will pulse weary far away exhausted. Nothing will ever again be able to reconstitute it I tell myself, but no matter how I stir the thought of the sadness that awaits me, it remains on the outside and colorless.

I say: shall I do your back? Monday morning. Ten o'clock. I've been writing for three hours. Docile modest my mother acquiesces. She extracts a tube of cream from her pocket. Had I not offered she would not have shown me the tube. She put the tube in her pocket. A traveler who packs for all contingencies. Submissive to the perhaps. – Shall I do you? She bows her head, she smiles, she brandishes the little tube. I do her back. Today I am doing the back of the human creature. Submission to the unknown laws of life. A pure and abundant light flows in the room and bathes the body, which glows. I see it all and I know nothing. What are these colors called, these dozens of reds of blue-blacks that lightly burnish the skin of the subject and shift with the combined pressure of the light waves and the minuscule quivering of the cutaneous folds? The left forearm is brick red who knows why. Three boils gape.

– They look like mouths, I say. *Des bouches.*

– *Des mouches?* Flies? My mother sounds scared. It's not black, is it?

– *Mouths*, I say. Pursed.

– Mouths?! You scared me! I don't see why I have this disease since it's incurable my mother says.

– It's for me, I tell myself. To recall me to my mother *in reality.*

I'll be this skin tomorrow.

– Today is July 14, says my mother. Bastille Day. I'm going to watch the parade.

– I'm going to see where our money goes says Eve Cixous. Two birds with one stone.

You can't tell her a thing, says my brother, brow furrowed, eyes sharp, the shopkeepers better watch their step, the butcher's bill, she studies it, her change she counts twice, old age: first the chromosomes get pruned, a necessary structure whose tips are trimmed says my brother, the kernel remains. The kernel of Mummy. She doesn't let herself be possessed.

– You've been possessed by that Montaigne.

No way to contradict her, I'd like to be in his possession but you might think quite the contrary.

– It was beautiful says my mother it was crazy, beautiful in one way crazy in another. Now we know where our money goes. Into the beautiful shoes, the beautiful trumpets. Women in skirts with different hats. Lots of dogs with tongues lolling out. Alsatians. I tell you it was unique superb, in color with white gloves, my mother glories. I'm not sure it is necessary. Beauty is expensive one can make do with less. But it was truly beautiful. But it's the State that underwrites all that and me. But everything marched in a perfectly straight line whereas here nothing works and everything is crooked.

– The shopkeepers says my brother are polite and kind. It's old age. No doubt about it. The shopkeepers are polite, Mummy rude. – Carrots! – How many would you like Madame? – She holds up five fingers. Saying the strict minimum. Never says thank you. They believe my mother is mute. Radishes! Bang goes the umbrella. It works like a charm.

Te lucis ante terminum,
rerum Creator, poscimus

ut pro tua clementia,
sis praesul et custodia.

What's that you're humming? A little Latin hymn to fend off ghosts and pollutions.

– July 14 doesn't interest you, where your money goes.

– I'm interested in July 15. Get up, I say, tip your head a bit. Three new boils on your shoulder. – You're off to the parade. She laughs. – We're going to Monoprix after for the cream.

– You want to buy cream at Monoprix?

– There are always different brands at Monoprix where you can park if you purchase something. The cream pays for the parking. She laughs. – But to park at Monoprix we have to cross the whole city. – You must park where the cream for the parking is and vice versa.

The more I anoint the more my mind adheres physically to the mysterious fabric of love.

– I am *décutie*. Worn thin. You know that word?

Décutie goes into my mother's word hoard along with cacochymy dowager Mathusalem. Because of old age we don't know a lot of words for old age, all I know is *Altersswäche ein Tattergreis.*

– A scrap for me. *Abfall.* That's the word. An old crust. A debris. There aren't a lot of them. An old dodderer. Falling to pieces, it's not typical. Deaf as a post, that I am.

And to top it off: *ein alte Schachtel.* An old cardboard box: you think it but you don't say it.

Leftovers, that are swept up and glued together.

I am your *alipte*, I say, I am your personal trainer and masseuse. I oil you.

But there's no ointment against the bad thoughts and phantasms.

I pause a moment to look up *Skin* in the Boissière dictionary. *Skin 1 cutis* and *pellis* in Latin; in Greek *derma* and *diphthera*; then *uter*, *utris*; and *ascos*. And *Skin 2* diseases of the skin of which there are hundreds.

On a desert island I would want the articles *Skin 1* and *Skin 2*. The poetry of persecutaneous persecution. Crumpled, crushed, rucks smocks grumpy sighwry scrunched-up scowling

Cutambulent that's what I am.

On skins I crawl, upside-down and inside-out, but I don't tell my whereabouts for my loves I would hide

Custom allots to the jailer the condemned man's belt and the old shirt above, to the hangman what remains below worn-out trousers skirt socks, but of all of us herein held who knows who's condemned to whose death. All of us are kept on the same terms. He who dies kills me, I kill myself to death, I am hand in hand with death I spend my days palpating it. You think it isn't contagious. But the soul that comes close enough to touch catches like a funeral pyre. You think it stays outside, it rolls its oceans up around the hips of our world, how else explain the immense anguish that blows in my face, great wind of winds, when before sun-up, before the hour of anointing my mother, I run to greet the Ocean, the eternal and savage world animal for the past forty years at the bounds of my thought. Down there on the beach re-beginnings where everything is washed clean each day nothing veils the scene of memory, no curtain, no television, no artifacts, no human fabrications, there is no time, only youth, virgin life and the canny woodcutting of nature. What loses its head, tree, you, or me, holds itself up, body simplified in the air, as my mother stands naked before my soul in hiding. The trunks: scoured by sea winds, licked, spit and polished to the point of turning into naked totems, to the point of deification.

This morning before sunrise I found myself with my brother on the crest of the mountain without a name which a hundred years from now will no longer exist – the dune was fifteen meters tall at birth says my brother, a hundred years ago nobody thought it would become the highest most beautiful Dune in Europe to begin with and later in the world we have known it in full ascension, we have watched it raise its golden, perfectly shaped head and become the wonder of the world, and this admirable dune has henceforth commenced its disappearance, in fifty years the forces of the winds and destiny will have annihilated it, all that will remain of this magnificent creature will be millions of photographs, luckily I tell myself we too will be in the state of photographs, this was the July 15, 2005, I was happy to feel life dwindling, the one-of-its-kind-dune-in-the-world is slipping out from under our feet, I sit on a stump in between two trunks deified to the bone, once giant pines, this place has such purity, thoughts of all ages press in along with memories of childhoods, of Algeria, of Montaigne, of Stendhal, of Derrida, of my friend the for-forever, Derrida again, of my Life ancient and modern with its heroes and its sages, past and to come, its tombs and its libraries. "When I think that we were standing the two of us on the top of the Dune," I will think, facing the Ocean of invisible promised events half vanished half alive, soon I will think, I was thinking, thinking not "Eve's waiting for us at the house" but "Eve's still waiting for us at the house," for death rose within me like the tide, I will soon think, I was thinking, I was in this scene and reliving it, I was *sur-viving* it, I was putting a gloss on it, I never came to the Dune with my beloved outside I was thinking, I never came here without my beloved *intus* and *in cute* each time I have come here with my brother I've had my beloved under the skin. Today is the first time that I've prelived this scene, I can feel myself telling myself: I *still* have him inside and in the skin, I can touch him touching me I could telephone him and I add to the heart of each thought of possibility this adverb of sufferance, the mysterious French *encore* – the *still*, the *yet* – for its ambiguous charms to which you have several times addressed poems in my language and yours.

I see perfectly the transparent white wall that marks the separation between my inner personal eras.

And what makes me see that I can see the white partition so clearly is the sudden, grandiose, brutal, unexpected setting off of an internal storm of supernatural size, whose cause I see perfectly but for which I was unprepared. The cause is July 15 a date to which I've given considerable thought these past few weeks, well aware that my friend's birthday was in the offing, sensing also the shadow of that day in the Vague Zone, a not so well-known programme, of the putting into memory of our mental apparatus, a kind of Sleep I notice in my cats whose timers are set for each and every hour of each and every day by all sorts of traces of abracadabra-esque punctuality. What I forget they remember. If one evening I were to forget to anoint my mother, the cats go and come and drag it in. I let nothing pass and I know nothing. I know and I am ignorant. Naturally I was expecting this July 15, I vaguely saw it approaching and time with its meanders kept me moving towards this familiar day with its store of delights and most likely in a good mood, being the birthday of so many beings beneficial and vital to me, among whom my Aunt Eri, the first of my adored cats and the day of the planting of the oak, to which since 1961 I am indebted for the peace without which I should never have been able to write and to which I owe so much and in a way so radical, necessary, ominously lucky, so gravely and therefore ridiculously religious that I have never in my whole life breathed it to a soul. It's as if it didn't exist. To this very day not only have I never breathed a word of it but I've never thought of mentioning it and perhaps never even thought of the arch-vital tree I planted forty-four years ago the way you plant a tree of life and death, believing and not believing, on the day I first crossed the threshold of the house built to shelter my son the mongoloid, in which as it turned out he never lived. I thought nothing. I planted. I hadn't yet met my friend J.D. I hadn't yet written my first book. I hadn't met my beloved. I was unborn. All these events took place some years later. Without the oak I could not have begun to write, as a consequence none of those events would have happened. Destiny's links remain hidden to us for at least forty years. Forty years, the length of a vital human blindness. Everything that turns out to have been decisive in the history of an individual or a people only shows its face after forty years in hiding. What I owe to this oak, had it been struck by lightning, uprooted, felled, by the Great Storm that killed nine hundred-year-old pines in the garden in the year 2000 and Montaigne's cedars, I would have cruelly recognized, but I stop. The oak goes on.

It's as if I hadn't said a thing.

Mum's the word. I awaited this July 15 which was coming once again, again, once, coming, everything has changed, the words do not change, nor the names, the July 15 which was coming this time, in the same place utterly different, would come, will come, would pass, will pass, its turn of the wheel on the heart, my mother also with her sister sick at heart, and not sick in the heart the way the doctors mistake it deceivers each and every time you consult them, they know nothing of the heart or the bodies or the cells, we know that, I was waiting for July 15, on the 14th I reread *Shibboleth*, in other words the book that comes time and again to sing of that which comes to reveal itself the one and only time. A book I know by heart and that I forget by heart as well. What good did it do? I don't know. I'll never know. While I was standing with my brother, with the two totemized trunks next to us, all of a sudden the Absolute felled me. It was nothing or anything. And without metaphors. An inner global collapse. The world *seemed* in appearance. Not a word. Not a word of silence. But the absolute exaltation of an anguish of monstrous dimensions, a monstrous excavation of the cellar of the soul, like an eruption of shadow but colorless, and manifest merely as tactile sensation. It is Absence that I Sense, I sensed, its gigantic body of feverish nothingness, its heap of storm pendant from the body of the world, lava without heat, ghost flows of lava through the biggest forest in Europe cavings-in of dunar sky to snuff out the tiny little heart left in my breast, the emptiness is a fullness without skin that makes the entire surface of the body with skin but without movement and fingerless, body crippled and tied in knots with horror, feel the crush of its exsufflated dilations. I felt distinctly, as in a dream, distinctly carnally spiritually death's presence within me, the dead and deading part inside my life, that which I had not understood seen suspected before, the concrete execution of the ablation of a bite of life in a being, nothing the least like an abstraction but a necrosion of obviously invincible force. It had been there for a few months, had dug for me by me into me, one represses the chasm, sets it aside, one doesn't suspect, one goes on living on the illusion of the separation of body and soul, of the wounds of the body and the wounds of the soul and above all of loss and the idea of it, of death and its being on the outside, whereas it bores into us, its hole and its hole-making, its killing and carving activity, and it's this brutal sensation-discovery of the teeth which are not going to stop biting, this sensation-discovery that what has happened is happening, the harrowing discovery that the uprooting is going to start over, as far as the imagination of time can take me, as if it were given me to catch a glimpse of the sum total of all the re-openings of wounds that will happen, thus to sense and moreover have a presentiment of, it's – as if from the top of the highest dune in the world in one glance I could survey the quantity of time in slices of sorrow coming my way – the internal vision of quantity in detail, a swarm of absences on the march, not a simple global and terminal Absence, but a procession, a future, it was this physical revelation of infinite repetition that

I could not bear and which I will have to notbear and bear, which gave off, on the spot, a precise gaseous equivalent of the catastrophe to come: furthermore, this splitting and precise pain at one point of my temporal body at the place of an amputation of an essential part of my vital mode, gushed with anguish that kept spreading and spreading, it's the soul I am losing, I told myself, all of a sudden I identified its contents. I had just realized I will never again in my whole life telephone my friend, that is to say, a certain essential thread or line of communication for my kind of being and my kind of writing has been irreparably cut. This of all lines. It is an awfully serious sentence for somebody like me: Thou shalt not telephone.

So that's what July 15 did to me. The day laid its finger on the place of *my* cut. When something awful happens you are flooded with suffering, pain, fear, loss of all forms. Among the brand-new and terrifying ills that buffet and blind us is *one main misfortune*. That misfortune is a summary, a mirror in the gut of the singular tie woven between two people, a signature of sorts, and the navel of the tale of which these people are the characters and agents.

So never again can I call my friend on the telephone and thereby flee in a second the place I am in, which I used to be able do at any moment, which I could do and did, the way one breathes for forty years, so naturally, so naturally I never said to myself "I am breathing" when I took a breath, and yet I do recall and do hear myself heaving a sigh of relief when he picked up, I thought it was a game and it was breathing itself,

every time I needed to get away from the place I was in, all I had to do was give him a call, and *voilà*! my flight was booked. This was the line that kept me alive for forty years wherever I happened to be, whatever the circumstances, whatever the capital cage, in with the rats of one or the other language, always on or under a table with a banquet of rats and sometimes confident that my constitutional need for flight was guaranteed I could stay wherever it was I seemed to be because if I urgently needed to get away from a place contrary to my nature or dangerous for my reason and above all my writing, something that happens a lot to me, all I had to do was phone him and without wasting a second, perambulatory remarks, sometimes hidden behind the tall draperies of a hotel dining room, sometimes in the toilets of a university building, sometimes from the concertina vestibule linking two coaches of a train, give him a description of the rodent environment, no difficulty criticizing my environment, no fear of exaggerating or of upsetting my interlocutor, I paint for him briefly, crudely, all that is base and platitude and sneering all that is hostile to the slightest shimmer of thought, all that fears and hates the idea of making thought vibrate in those societies that are predisposed to thought, that despise and scorn it the minute it moves those commissions, those colleges, those departments, those conservatories of arrogance and incompetence whose members virtually one hundred percent failures fear the very subject of their profession inasmuch as it is noble and whose only care is to degrade their subject and to execrate those who cherish it. I would telephone him and I was no longer wherever I was, I didn't take my friend by surprise, who often found himself in similarly detestable society and each time, hundreds of times, that my execration of the ongoing state of evil in the heart and the indigestion was at its peak I could telephone him, therefore, sure of this possibility I didn't abuse it, I could be satisfied with the thought of phoning him or with phoning him virtually in the middle of a banquet of colleague rats, for instance, or during the lecture of a sometimes famous therefore even rattier Rat, when I was at the height of execration – unlike Stendhal who at the height of Grenobloise execration had no one to telephone – I saw myself calling him, I could picture the life-saving act, I would say: "I'm in Grenoble," and the insurance policy took effect, I knew he would understand and recognize my state of revulsion, which sufficed to enable me to stay on in reality where in truth I was not. "I'm in Grenoble," I would say if I was in Frankfurt, he might be in "Grenoble" too, a city to which I've never been and him either, and sometimes I could say "in Gre-," or maybe "in Gran," or "Square Gre-" it was a murk of the stinky streams of *Granges* filled with *grenouilles-frogs* under a film of green rot, of Grenette and Grève Square, I would say *gre* for the disgust, the hellishness, the death sentence, the base. As a result I owe even my academic career, which during the forty-three years that I have wallowed in it has never ceased to cause me disgust, indignation and revolt, to the coverage of this insurance policy which allows me to pick up the phone and call him, which has been the constant source of my strength hidden even from myself. Imagine Carthage stocked with water, oil, munitions by underground supply lines and an ingenious network of invisible cisterns, imperturbably facing Rome utterly convulsed by the tremors and shocks of the death wish. All those years I could be transported whenever I wished, the minute I was home I could be not there, the minute I was out, flight was guaranteed, I didn't even need to telephone, I had the possibility.

While I climb the Dune with my brother, it comes to me suddenly that I've lost unhappiness along with happiness, the happiness of the unhappiness whose name for decades was Grenoble, the word Grenoble which was odious has now been charged with a fearful sweetness.

Now on the Dune I can see I had an all-risk Coverage. Even, I tell myself, I owe my romantic novels, that is my infernal paradises, to this ever-present escape hatch which allowed me, paradoxically, more than once to stay around beyond what was reasonable, in impossible situations albeit furnished with attractions as most aberrations are, or sure of my Possibility and my Privilege I could always let myself stray off beyond the bounds of what is reasonable and tolerable, the incredible importance of which I didn't fully appreciate, nobody around me myself included being in on the secret, nor had anyone of my near and dear, my family, those closest to me, ever been able to understand. I could sink to the depths of execration of the state of the heart's evil from which I could make my escape with one little phone call, on which I never acted.

And it is the extraordinary immensity of this utterly unique and irreplaceable possibility whose longevity alone had made manifest its powers and absolute singularity which appeared to me for the first time to me in the form of an immense and diffuse death anguish oozing out as if bottomless in scarves of haze around the forest's thousands of trunks, a phenomenon that could not concretely have occurred had I not found myself on the top of the highest Dune in the world, on that particular day. Place allows and decides about our passions and our works. Without Mount Janicule unique in the world no Henry Brulard.

If I went onto the Dune to let my unsuspected inner tornado hit me with the required force, it was completely unawares and not my doing. Lately I desire nothing I traipse after my brother, the tragic centers of interest which make him burst out laughing, it's not me who would like to choose, wait to look for, indicate, I follow along. I have enough problems when it comes to scaling the heights just lifting one leg and then the other.

We are on the top of the Dune which has never been so high and which in fifty years will be merely a pack of postcards without any interest for us who will be merely a pack of snapshots I was thinking and yet this huge anguish that ghosts the world scares me as if 1) I believed it immortal 2) hence as if I believed myself immortal 3) whereas if there is one thing I know for sure it is that I'm not, because my mother isn't.

It is only today that I can see before me the bizarreness of my life that I have always believed to be single, but which goes in two's as you could in theory note in the scene in which I am alone with my brother on the top of the Dune, with my brother as always when I am alone, I mean in the absence of my love, alone in a mild solitude, for my brother is the only being who does not in the least interrupt my solitude, it's innate, we are so congenital so made that we can say everything saying nothing, and when we walk side by side arm in arm, hand in hand, it changes nothing, we only unfold and rearrange the body's two parts, the being composed of two hinged parts, very different but the combination is stable, wends its way, each wends her way, each his own, each thinks of his love her novel his plot and subplot and knows not what he she lends the other. One of the oldest and most confidentially fraternal –in every sense – uses to which I have put my brother has always been to stand in for my love especially in vetting places which I am considering as backdrops, scenery or objects of encounters which require perfection and for which my brother can pose without any risk of devaluation. All the same I have never used my brother as a stand-in for my friend in the phone department for there can be no doubling or advance preparations in the case of this operation reduced to its simplest, without staging,

My life is therefore now here? It pains me the idea of being unable to want to call my friend, I've never done this and I didn't suffer, I have always kept separate the roles and attributions, never would I have confided my fits of anger and anxiety to a being so distant from the scenes, so foreign to their artificial exiles and idiom, this is neither ethical nor economical. It pains me the idea of not being able to call my friend up on the phone. Before wherever I was in danger, I was at the same time on the phone, this was natural. And now I can feel by subtraction the incredible importance of this, thus I believed natural being-elsewhere, when in fact it was practically supernatural. I realize to what extent there's no elsewhere. I can't call my mother

With my mother flight is impossible. I can't call her 1) she is deaf. Trying to talk to my mother on the phone, which brings me to the brink of despair, I avoid. Trying to talk to her is another planet, a non-sense, it is an instant of separation which I am incapable of putting up with and that she puts up with very well; 2) she is here. She is even the Here-and-Now in person.

II

BENJAMIN'S BED

– Get up, I say.

– We're going to do the cream cheese, says my mother.

I say: unction, she says: cream cheese.

A creased, crumpled, crinkly, tucked, puckered and gathered time, everything twofold, "when I was a girl" says my mother, her body shrunken supple flexible fold turn bend under the floppy shift of crinkly, twisted, kinky skin. Perfect little buttocks, all the old age is in the corkscrew legs.

I am afraid of the legs.

These days my mother laughs often, more and more often, explosive laughter. She snorts with laughter, she laughs herself to tears, at length, alone.

My mother's two legs. What doesn't hold up. Twin towers, scratched, crackly, pitted cratered veined. I'm afraid of the towers the two towers with their bulging blistered ulcerated varicose veins

Before-the-death-of-Mummy, a time with no beginning where one finds oneself troubled, gaze cut off. The body-veil lets the Other show through

– They were forever fleecing me, says my mother, one time Germany, one time my father's brother, one time Algeria. She gives a cackle of laughter that remembers, remembers – remembers. I go on polishing, irritated, she primps, I shine her hips.

Once – and once only – she didn't get fleeced, it's the business of the bed that makes her laughlaugh.

– I've heard this one before – I'm about to cut her off annoyed. – Have I told you this story before? the laugher asks, anxiously. – No, I've never heard it. – Well she chuckles it was all because of a bed and without that bed you wouldn't be here.

And I submit to the bed. *Sommier*, a pure gold word.

– In Paris with Eri she was fun to be with, I took the initiatives and Eri tagged along, there was a lot of to-ing and froing in those days, refugees

one day Eri and I were with a group of refugees I heard somebody was leaving, a certain Mr Benjamin, he's in the midst of moving, the apartment almost bare, people are always on the move,

– Have you sold everything? – All that's left is the bed, a few plates, some books. – I'll take them. (Now) I had a bed. Mr Benjamin's bed where to leave it? We leave it with the concierge. – Which Mr Benjamin? I say. – I'm going to tell you. Now I have a bed, I need to find an apartment says my mother. I was working in Romainville behind the Porte des Lilas there are lots of new buildings, this was on the Boulevard Mortier, a new building going up, yes, I rent a modern two-room flat with shower. Off I go to collect my bed. Your bed? the concierge tells me I gave it, that dead-loss piece of junk, to the first peddler that came along. I go to see Mr Benjamin. Don't worry I'll come with you. My mother acts the concierge, Mr Benjamin, Eri and her sister my mother, the refugees, the imaginary peddler, she even does the *sommier*-bed, that *dead-loss piece of junk* according to the concierge and according to Mr Benjamin a bed with a good many years of use left in it. Benjamin, I say, did he have glasses? My mother does the glasses. Right away you notice. He had glasses. Polite, an intellectual. We go to pick up the bed and what do you know? it's back. I have the bed moved to my flat. You still have it down in Arcachon. I had a little Hungarian refugee make a mattress for it. A wardrobe a table shelves therefore with books. – The bed in the downstairs bedroom? – Your brother's room. – Which books? – Now all I need is a rug and some chairs. I go to the Galeries. I find just what I want. – Is all this going to fit? I say. And it's all still down in Arcachon. And there you have it, a beautiful apartment. What else did I need? says my mother. Whoops! says my mother. Look at that! We bend to look.

A big blister on her left foot. That's a new one, says my mother. The nails: varnished brick red. Eri made curtains. We wrote to Omi in Osnabrück who sent us some thick velvet Eri made the ruffle on the dark green bedspread. Would you believe I took all those pieces of furniture to Arcachon? She chuckles. I stare the eye of the Cyclops in the face. On his brow a crown of brick red toenails. Who can look death in the eye? says my friend. For a long time. My mother laughs. She spins out her life. Staring into the eye of the Cyclops I get hypnotized, it's reciprocal, I've got death by the eye I myself am inoculated, soul standing guard, watchdog asleep. Several chapters go by. I come back just before the young doctor who is to become my father. He arrives in Paris from Algiers. Pauline from Oran gave him the address of the people I rented a room from says my mother. In those days no telephone. One Sunday he turns up there and nobody. Luckily the concierge had our address. One Sunday and it was on the other side of town where he had to take the metro all the way East and him all the way West. One of life's little flukes says my mother. To find those girls in a very pretty apartment must have impressed him. All that, as you know, counts. Life, says my mother. And everything still in Arcachon. Those rush-seated chairs that looked like they'd never last. Chairs, chairs, where is my father. And all because of the bed.

– You never told me it was Benjamin's bed.

– I totally forgot. She bursts out laughing. She laughs for a while. One of life's flukes. She laughs while I, face to face with the Cyclops, think about the flukes of forgetting and of memory. Today is July 15 I'd forgotten Benjamin is July 15 too. I think: should I regret learning the secret of the bed so late, too late or maybe not or should I be glad that I've never known that my brother has been dreamlessly sleeping for forty-four years on Benjamin's bed that my mother forgot about or should I be astonished with either joy or pain that the bed outlasts the man, the chairs live on, my father long dead. I can't tell my friend this story, these days no telephone. I might have thrown the bed away, my brother's been complaining for decades about how uncomfortable it is, what kept me from it, what force, one of life's little flukes, a formula which remains secret – who knows?

– I note, says my mother. She's finished laughing.

– You laugh at forgetting it? Or at remembering?

She doesn't know what makes her laugh. That's what makes her laugh. – I'm laughing because whenever I tell you a story you always think you've heard it before.

My utter exasperation yesterday, for the twentieth time in two months, teeth on edge, it's the third time in the space of two days I've heard this one, sumptuous tales, modest chefs-d'oeuvre and rich in lessons, it set my teeth on edge, my mother over the years has become an artist, now she interprets her tales, she does different voices, she brings them to life, she acts all the parts, I couldn't wait for it to be done, I painted a look of attention on my face, I was invaded the telephone no longer rang, I couldn't flee, I was more and more criminal, yet I listen every evening to Schumann's *Symphonische Etüden* without gnashing my teeth, for the twentieth time as if it were the first, I listen for hours on end to the same Beethoven sonatas that are not the same, when my mother says: "that reminds me," I have but one thought in my head: make her stop. I hear "*Çamrappelle* thatremindsme" and right away I'm on the rack. She says *çamrappelle* every chance she gets, she's always on the lookout for a chance to beremindedof tales and anecdotes. Every morsel is a pearl, a treasure of humanity. A robot. My mother beams. She shows off her strong points, she marches out her regiments, her brasses, her polished duds it's all perfect, it's beautiful, but the inner me hasn't the possibility to revel in it, only a frantic impossibility. On the other hand I haven't the moral permission to shout: Enough! For my mother it is indispensable and vital to *çamrappeler* two or three times a day, at meals and during the unction, to check, that is, the state of her psychic functions and at the same time revisit and repeat the story of her life and thereby be surprised all over again by life's little flukes, for, and this is the key to her artistry, it's not that she remembers, it's that the thing *comes back* to her, the facts recur at the moment she invokes them, they turn up again, they come along to happen to her, brand new occasions to revel in. And this because 1) she has forgotten everything 2) *out of the blue* she remembers, and what bliss it is to be and to have been alive in those days that don't look a day older.

I try not to hear, but I can't, I don't listen to her; but she comes through loud and clear, naturally I can't plug my ears, I know very well that I am not me for her I am not me and I am not me the one she is speaking to nor am I the person she would like to be speaking to, I am merely the person at hand, on the spot, if she had her choice, she'd pick a virgin, I am replaceable and I do my best to get replaced, I yield my place to my daughter, to my brother, to one of our children and grandchildren, not for a second does she pretend it is to me she speaks, quite the contrary, but I can't always find someone else when I need them.

At the same time I want to stay, I want to hear every last one of my mother's words, she whom I love more than myself I want to hold on to every instant, I want to keep the unbearable exasperation, I want to remember right now, this very minute and for the time of times, each modulation of my mother's voice, each of the hundreds of daily images of my mother, I want to record instantaneously mentally each intolerable prick of my being-with-mummy, I want to have a simultaneous indelible double of everything that composes the life and work of my mother from the nail polish slapped on her big toe that has been dogging me ever since I learned to crawl, to the divinely awkward smiles my mother chastely sets on lips grown impossible to draw, I don't want to lose a crumb of everything I need to flee and to sweep away

I can see myself weeping later on soon for everything that this morning gets on my nerves, this very day I am jealous of today I am filled in advance with regret for the scene I'd like this instant to exit from, in advance I regret each of the distressing feelings that troubles me in this scene in which I feel trapped and in which I will later and in vain want to be trapped again as in a dream. I reject and I regret. I'll so want still to be able to reject and regret rejecting, and it will be in vain. Even if they promised me "the Benefits of the Bed" I thought then, in the old days – that is, today July 15 – I've never had the gift of panning for gold even if I hoped to happen on the precious nugget that had miraculously escaped the sifting and resifting, I'm incapable of drawing from this feeble hope the stony thickness of a kind of patience, that's what I thought on that July 15 I will think in 2011, I will be leafing through the notebook Bibliothèque Nationale BN Pentateuch Egypt 1353 MSS Department in which I wrote the notes "summer 2005 mother and daughters" (i.e. my mother my daughter, me, three daughters therefore, mothers and daughters for one another in turn) I'll be enchanted, I'll be taken six years back in time that is yesterday, that is today, during these pages times will go and come without any difficulty for a few quarters of an hour I will no longer be in 2011 it will be July 15, 2005, a sort of wholly resuscitated present for I note the wholeness of the world as it palpitates in a spherical volume about two hundred meters in diameter, in the background the reciprocal coo-ings of the doves, in the foreground a dash of chirps, in the center of the world and the picture The Oak with its Superior People, the Mocking Squirrel People, everywhere on earth and in the trees the choir of cats going about their business, the large vase of sunflowers that my mother arranges for me, a chaste love offering made every year to the daughter a trophy, I'll hear the so ancient news of the presence of *Benjamin's Bed* which all unawares has been sleeping on the ground floor for forty-four years and which stirs up in my head and heart a soup of marvelously sad affects, for here is an archi-unexpected example of the effect of *sero te amavi*, that formula of Regret which my friend introduced to world thought in 1995, at a period when with regard to the *seroteamavi* effect – which had always existed but in the shadow and impotency that keeps a feeling of chagrin in a state of ghostliness, that of the thing without a name – it had become urgent, obvious, that here all of suffering humanity lacked the illumination of a name, people suffered from suffering from a state of mind without the name that lessens the sensation of madness, there were days when everybody felt the sudden weight of a nameless melancholy, at least in our culture and our language, and it is to my friend that we owe the expression, so gently so strongly saddened but so singingly, so appropriate for so many circumstances of modern misery. As Stendhal for *fioriture* sometimes one has to go and find the names for the orphan thing in another language, and the state, henceforth designated, retains from its foreign origin something of the enigmatic and the unrecognizable that the affliction kindles in us. The stroke of genius of my friend when in 1995 he crowned the expression *sero te amavi* is twofold: it lies in having sensed that the specter of an unqualified regret lurked in the contemporary soul; then having, so as to try to think it through, picked up a trace of this type of damage in the *Confessions* of Saint Augustine, in which, in a totally different context and situation, a similar sort of pain, gathered into the Latin word *sero*, expressed itself; and thereupon his having taken a sample of a fragment of a sigh from the depths of the ancient body with its immortal passions. You can't imagine a more infinite expression of the feeling of human finitude, than my friend's *sero te amavi*, now, like so many of his verbal discoveries, part and parcel of the human patrimony. If anyone asked me how to sum up the pains of solitude, I'd cite the citation *sero te amavi*. The Great Citer's gesture of successfully citing is in itself part of that delicate state of lamentation in which weeping and celebration mingle. The citation resuscitates, but in words, only in words, that is in spirit, the brazier that was, and only the citation has the power to seem to resuscitate, that is to render to what is gone the permission and the appearance of return. When, in 2011, I cite my friend he'll be back, I'll echo what he wrote in 1995, the echo being of course the continuation of the speech whose absence is momentarily suspended.

In 2011 I'll think therefore, at one and the same time, of my mother gallivanting about Paris in 1934 with her French "bed" in such a way that a few years later I was to be conceived from that very bed, of my stupefaction, caused by a repressed joy combined with a feeling of *sero te amavi* upon hearing on this July 15 of the unsuspected existence under my own roof, reposing under my brother, of a literary treasure; of my friend to whom naturally I'd that very day have told of this unlikely discovery that he, no doubt, would have absorbed with a sigh of admiration, mmmurmuring: "What a mystery! And to think that the entire summer of 2001 I busied myself with Benjamin's bed." Upon which, I'll think, he couched his own dreams of dreams, his hopes and his fears, his texts scintillating with the bright colors of anguish, bright blue, bright red, white. And at the same time of my friend to whom I'll not have recounted the story of the bed. At the same time of my mother, of my friend, of when I was happy, and when I still lived lives. That's what I thought in 1995 and in 2005, I'll think in 2011, but I see in my notebook that I was already thinking from time to time briefly but fearfully of what for me lay in the offing and hidden behind the curtain of time I'll think.

Time, my friend would say, I was thinking this July 15, I was thinking more than ever that day and above all of that word, time: "*Le temps*, time" that my friend must have spoken hundreds of times in my hearing, always with the same uncertain voice, colored as if with a shade of veneration, though we preferred the word *awe*. *Time* he would say his soul bowed to the "divinity," the most hidden entity therefore the most divine, the face of the soul turned towards the divinitude of the secret face, the force neither visible nor invisible whose name he uttered as one strikes a flint, watching out for all the signs and all the physiognomies all the looks of faces and figures of beings hallmarking partitions there was: Time, he discerned and greeted it, lived the world in its entirety as a temple of Time, "*Le Temps*" he would say in French voice groping, fingers spread and uncertain. *Le Temps*, its name in French, with the definite article, as if one knew what one doesn't know. I'll think.

During the unction that morning I told my mother Eve: "*Tu es le temps* – you are time, killing time." I'll find these words again in 2011 and howl silently, I noted on that July 15 in the days of Mummy.

This morning she was old, this happens, a shard of anger against the enemies, suddenly she grows old and enemies are hidden in each person and each chair, she fights back, she comes to her defense, she cries: next they'll put me on a leash and I'll be a dog. Just as I too by force of attraction reach the canine point, I restrain myself. Afterwards we forgot. I'll be a dog on a leash tomorrow. Afterwards, around 11 o'clock, she was again the Great Goddess of Time.

"The Time of the cat," I try to imagine Thessie's time my friend would say. I imagine his attempts to imagine the Time of the cat. The Time of the cat is not the Time of the dog. For an hour this morning my mother having got up in a bad mood found herself on a leash in the Time of the dog.

Occasionally there's leash between us. I imagine a technician, he'd record our grunts and groans. Mother and daughter going on a hundred years.

What's the good of having come across Benjamin's Bed now, I was thinking, all it does is stir up Regret, I tell myself, but it comes to me that the misery of Regret in these topsy-turvy times is a kind of happiness.

If I've happened on Benjamin's Bed it's an accident that might *never have occurred*, as it never has for thirty-three years, that is since my mother, hounded out of Algeria in 1971, stripped of all her worldly belongings, inaugurated in retaliation the age of total recall. I now have in the house, in which, all unsuspecting, I have been writing for over forty years, Benjamin's Bed. A Bed that's escaped the most tragic of fates.

To be the indirect descendent of Benjamin via the bed is for somebody like me an extraordinary piece of luck. By the bed especially, I tell myself. I set the bed over all other pieces of furniture, naturally. A good thing I didn't hear earlier. Who knows I tell myself if I wouldn't have given in to the temptation to sleep on this *sommier*-bed that over the years has borne with my brother's laborious dozing-and-wakings: his *sommes*.

Who knows what would have happened 1) to my relationship with my brother 2) from the addition of the ghost of an inheritance between us 3) with regard to the desirable or undesirable obsessions that this or that bed or bedding may cause a person who is particularly susceptible to phantasms of all sorts which, unlike my mother, I am 4) I envisage the hypothesis of a thesis on Benjamin instead of a thesis on Joyce 5) a bed of this sort would necessarily have modified all the real and imaginary structures of my life in all private and public domains 6) I wouldn't have been me 7) the blow of the bed – recognized – would have put me in debt, I'd have owed who knows what to Benjamin, whereas I owe nothing literarily to anyone save for predecessors and contemporaries declared as such by me. I would therefore have been dispossessed and altered in an improbable and incalculable way. For one thing, who knows how I would have reacted to the eschatological and apocalyptical upwelling of Benjamin in the work and thought of my friend. In what different manner and manners I'd have received and read the first version then the second of a phosphorescent text destined to be read before an immense assembly in Frankfurt in 2001 on the occasion of his being awarded the Adorno Prize, and which is now renowned and admired the world over as a more than philosophical, more than literary chef d'oeuvre, I have no idea. Everybody knows that this speech, which first received and then took for eternity the name of *Fichus*, and which is not a speech but under the appearance and appellation of "speech," a Supernatural Reverie, in appearance and duly addressed to Theodor Adorno, contains in truth an immense heartrending and lacerated love letter to Benjamin c/o Adorno. This love letter to Benjamin veiled by the speech in homage to Adorno is an example of *sero te amavi*, hence a true love letter, arriving like all love letters too late, like the love letter transformed into supreme book that the narrator was never to address to Albertine, a letter which had to wait for it to be too late twice over before it could begin to grow and grow until it attained the disproportion of a work of art. Later on, readers will wonder for what reasons, what causes conscious or unconscious, J.D. will have begun to write to Benjamin in July 2001 then gone on drafting such a letter till the eve of September 11, 2001, in such a way in Time, and in the times of Benjamin, of J.D. and of the world, that this twin-towered letter, by a vital ruse addressed by J.D. to Benjamin via Adorno to Adorno for Benjamin to the two friends and relations one of them already knocked down by fate the other still on his feet, was to receive from fate the imprint and reminder of that tragedy. As if J.D. had been served warning that a new catastrophe would take place at the instant and date of his writing, so very late, to Benjamin, about the catastrophe that Benjamin could not begin to imagine to which everything was leading him in the dark, of which he knew nothing save in terror and in dreams.

There's still no explanation. There's not always an explanation. At the very moment J.D. sends Benjamin, who wasn't expecting it, who hadn't ever expected it, the unhoped-for, despaired-of true answer to the letter written by Benjamin after a night on the straw, the letter of a dream of a night on a dream of some bedding, a letter which was to wander, solitary, knocking at door after door for sixty years, forever desperately waiting to be read, pure letter forever incapable of dreaming of being read as it was read eventually too late, but read to perfection all the same, which is to say read to tears for, reading it so late, even so late, tears came to J.D.'s eyes, a letter more beautiful than any other letter, the sum-*somme* of a dream of a letter and of eternity, the *somme*-sum of a dream letter and a dream eternity, and read to the letter as a sur-letter, letter for letter-being of genius, not yet arrived, letter-being which Benjamin remembering Stendhal can play at dreaming, on his pallet of straw, as if taking delivery of those traces a hundred years after the postmark date, a letter in cipher entrusted to Time beyond the October 12, 1939 lettereverie of reality, fingerprints of Persephone of speech destroyed,

at that very moment, the planes of the death of the Century took off for Adorno's birthday, September 11, as if Death were privy to all the Century's thoughts and knew what it doesn't know

There is an author, I tell myself, there has to be an Author, I don't know him, but you see how it's written, Time, the times, there's an *auteur*, an *ôteur*, a plotter and deleter: no sooner do we tie our knots than he undoes and redoes them.

– Back comes the bed like a charm, says my mother

– Benjamin? I say

– I saw him two or three times I didn't even know he was an author, those people were nobodies, the repatriated, says my mother of people who hadn't a thing as foreigners they had no rights. In those days there was a lot of coming and going, people coming from Germany, others going away again. It was a metal bed a sort of barbecue with little springs, I had moved into that apartment in which there was nothing and that was the first thing. *Sommier*, in German? Back in Germany we didn't have such things we had horse hair mattresses, they were firm you put them on a board.

With *sommier* I began life in France where nothing was modern, no such thing as a shower where I lived. *Sommier* I think it's where you *somme*. Snooze. *Sommier* French word. *Fremdwörter*, says my mother, you know that. What could be more German than this expression, what could be more German that this German double-barreled *Fremdwörter* word. Foreign words. *Sommier* French foreign word. In the two letters they exchange in French, J.D. and W.B., the one responding to the other responding to each other over a distance of sixty-two years, the note of disastrous happiness rings out. Each responds to the anguish of the other the letter of October 12, 1939 responds in advance to the letter of September 11, 2001, happiness in the disaster disaster in the happiness, who can say if the happiness is the foreigner or if it is the disaster?

I'm going to reread Benjamin's correspondence from the point of view of the *Sommier*, I tell myself, that is, from the point of view of the mattress and from the point of view of the one who sleeps on it.

That's when I turned around to look at the shelves on which are couched the Prousts, the Derridas, the Rousseaus, the Flauberts, the Stendhals I lay out flat as a horizon-line behind my back whereas "the Germans" I stand bolt upright in front of me the Celans the Sachs the Bernhards, some lying down the others standing up except for Montaigne always standing upright in front of me, I don't know why, and I couldn't find the two volumes of Benjamin's correspondence, these disappearances horrify me, lately a third of my life has been reduced to nothingness by Disappearances. Naturally the books and papers to which I am particularly, passionately even, attached are the ones that go missing under my eyes, I spend hours hunting for them, is the world leaving me or am I myself leaving? Either that or they haven't disappeared and I'm the one who can't find them just when all of a sudden I can't go on living without them

When my brother comes to visit, I barely give him time to sit down on the palaver armchair before I ask him what he thinks of Benjamin, Walter Benjamin I say.

– Who's Walter Benjamin?

– For forty-four years you've been sleeping on Walter Benjamin's bed I say.

– Move me, says my brother.

– I move him at length. At the time of the letter, the immortal one, you were a year old I say. Right after that it's "*total uncertainty*." Uncertainty with the certainty that the hour that rang in his ears for the first time on the straw is soon going to be ringing for the last time.

– That metal bed she and Daddy used to sleep on? The chairs too? – Only the Bed. She brought it all this way, I say. – Don't kid yourself. It isn't because of its symbolic value. It's because of Mummy's practical side.

– You felt nothing? I feel out my brother

– I always thought that bed was dreadful.

When the two volumes of the *Correspondence* I ordered to replace the missing ones finally turn up, because of an archaic superstition I go to my brother's room to unwrap them, I sit on the bed with its dreadful springs, I open them the way you draw cards and right away I find the Bed. "Dear Grete, it's taken me a while to write back to you this time – but also how much has happened between your first letter and today. Above all, another move – then some private difficulties, though of the most ordinary kind and, in just the sort of situation to provoke it, a revolt of objects in all directions starting, since I live on the seventh floor, with an elevator strike, next, the sweat pouring off me, moving the bed down to the concierge, followed by a massive migration of some rags I am attached to, and culminating in *the disappearance* of a very fine pen, for me irreplaceable. A true disaster."

I write you, he writes, without having found it. I write these lines on the table facing the pile of volumes to which I am so attached as to live in fear of their *disappearance*, *one only loses what one can't replace* I tell myself. Once the irreplaceable has gone, one goes on losing the irreplaceable. The loss of the irreplaceable is followed by a massive perdition, summoned up by dolor, everything to which I seem attached vanishes, I tell myself,

I write this with the writing pen my friend left me, a fearful pen that I finally decided not to take on trips for fear of compulsively forgetting it in one of those dangerous foreign hotels where one *must* lose some essential object, you stay in those dangerous hotels when you are invited to speak to a well-meaning crowd on subjects that ought to remain confidential, grave, personal subjects, such as art or adoration, of which you must both speak and not speak, each time I'm in a situation of uncertainty, I must lose some precious object, of no commercial value, but of a value on the spiritual level all but unavowable. I'll be able to make a book of the *Missing Objects* in all the countries in the world where my love and I have stayed together. The last of the Missing Objects *forever and ever* irreplaceable was in New York two years ago, my Fortuny I called it. The description: a very plain white night-gown, nothing fancy, hand-washable, about the weight of an envelope, and which has been with us for over twenty years. I only wore it on our trips and therefore hardly ever, a negligee a nothing that over the years took on the secret nobility of a sacred linen. This was in the Gramercy Park Hotel, unfortunately. Our hotel. The second evening the minute I entered it was no longer there, I saw it. I had a token struggle with the management. No one denied. It seems only two night-gowns vanish every day, a small proportion for five hundred guests. The Housekeeping Service offered me three other white nightgowns, forgotten or stolen. This gown I said for me evokes Venice, Prague, Rome, Edinburgh, Cambridge, Bombay, the desire to go there, the anguished happiness of having been there, the fear of returning and of not returning, and it is not merely the nightdress, it's the whole Hotel, and dozens of moments followed by poems, I said, I cried, I went crazy. And the disaster? I cried, I saw the end approaching, first our towers and then our Fortuny. To think I called it Fortuny. The unwear-out-able, the invincible. It was as if they'd stolen my skin. It was like losing your one and only fountain pen. Will I ever write again, will I ever write what I was going to write, how to interpret the sign, in what aura of fatality does my hand move on the paper the pen that will never be the missing one? Everything can be replaced, nothing can be replaced. Never again will I be me thinks Benjamin. He may have lost the fine pen while he was carrying the sold Bed down. Who knows what he would have written had he not sold that bed to my mother?

In 1936 the bed arrived in Oran.

"And we can run as often as we like to all the windows, writes the new pen, everywhere the weather is dismal" (July 1937).

Even if it's too late, the desire to tell the story of the bed's survival to my friend. It's come down to him

A bed that almost never woke up.

– Losing is all that's left, I say.

– Losing is all we've got left to lose, you say

The impossibly of not telling, I cannot do otherwise, one can only tell otherwise, with always the same need to make sense of what you've lost, the need not to lose this feeling of losing, the need to feel yourself not losing this feeling that you are still losing the irreplaceable.

The weather turns threatening and we run to all the windows.

So long as she is alive, I tell myself, I've lost nothing yet of all that I've lost. Right now I am doing her chest from the neck down. Once and only once she didn't get fleeced, which was that metal mattress, that bed from which everything started in 1935 then in 1936, whereas for Benjamin the chain of events was the reverse in 1937, he had less and less space, having given up his former lodgings, had he been able to join up with the bed in Algeria, instead of ending up on straw in the camp in the Nievre, but he was never to know that his *sommier*-French-word outlived him, first in Oran, then Algiers, then Paris then in this book. I'm going to leave this bed to someone in my will I mused but to whom? To whom donate an inestimable and unique bed, whose springs are tired to death, discontinued model, not worth a penny, which was, for having been sold lost forgotten shipped, at the untold origin of sumptuous and sinister nights on straw and of pages, in color, of dreams among the loveliest of the century that we've left behind us, allowing it, at the age of a hundred, to sink slowly under time along with its inhabitants, with no final resting place other than the flimsy shelter of a volume of letters. When I am no longer here who will take in the bed? Had I only known earlier, it might, entrusted to my friend J.D., have been incorporated into his book *Fichus* alongside its former master and have had a share of the immortality along with the straw, the hat, the blue-trimmed sail, all those *minima* that make the principal Fichu of this brilliant tender delicate memorial a funeral cortege of small secondary lost objects such as are found in Egyptian tombs. But it seems fortune has held off until it is one day too late for me to save Benjamin's bed. Without these familiar beings, pots, mirrors, ladles, cats, and other such brought from home to keep them company, the dead would be lost, terrified by death, tormented by the prospect of the voyage to the foreign land, as Benjamin felt himself more vulnerable than ever to History's attacks when he no longer had his pen as sacred reservoir to protect him, reservoir of the world, a world in itself, pocket world, sword or revolver, and as secret figurine, statue and double of its master. Benjamin had even lost sight of the loss of the bed. But the bed for its part was deprived of origin and kin, it had dragged around a soul-less survival of house-removal debris. Still, there'd been a mysterious limit to the status of unknown bed, I observe: as if there was in the bed a residue of inexplicable "force," something invisible and intangible around or in the bed that always set aside the aggressive impulses that haunt our household, a sort of secret strength, lodged in the metal perhaps or perhaps in the vague idea of venerable age, which kept at bay the idea of ridding ourselves of a white elephant of a piece of furniture, cumbersome, uncomfortable and as if a wordless pity in the form of neglect kept watch over the carcass, none of us could ever bring ourselves to take the bed to the dump. None of us ever analyzed this. None of us ever noticed the endurance of the bed, or its existence even. No brutal anger against the bed or myself as the one responsible for his insomnias ever assailed my brother. We neither chased it away nor took it apart nor put up with it. Nor did we revere it, oil it, pat it. None of us ever gave it a thought. It lay there. I imagine its suffering, if it has a soul, as being similar to that of an old mother-in-law who keeps herself busy in the kitchen enveloped in a silence beneath which she shuts up a terrified prayer: may I not be sent to the hospice. As the part of the bed the least visible furthest removed from the fabrics and the body you might say the bedframe occupied the lowest, humblest place, I tell myself and I didn't hide from myself the sadness of my feeling of sympathy for old servants, grandmothers aging valets forgotten in the cherry orchards, all those old brooms beings of which my mother says: *Alte Bäsel pfegen auch*. The old brooms still sweep but we sweep them out. What's a bedframe? It is as yet unthought. Wretched I am for everything that has not yet been thought and that only my friend could have thought. What's in a bed, this thing that's not the mattress, this purely occidental object, and not even German, the forgettable par excellence, the support, but also the frame? The parergon. And yet, I tell myself, the bedframe, the humble, the un-wear-out-able the metallic, who will swear it hasn't a soul? Who will say what quantity of soul is containable and contained in its frame its corners, its springs, its empty space?

And what shall I say of its durability when in the present case the bed's longevity exceeds that guaranteed by the industrially manufactured object?

Perhaps usage in this case has signed a pact with *Ur*-age? Such-and-such a line of beds manufactured in France of imported German steel, that is supposed to have been W. Benjamin's bed, has it not acquired some original value, some melancholy perfume of a sort as yet unstudied by chemistry, that adheres to the metal? For the bed remembers, like the old broom, or the unbreakable old woman. As for its esthetic value, this depends on me. On my gaze. On the way my skin, my surface, my depths receive the traces of twentieth-century history as it was lived and recorded by this bizarre machine with its cork-screw vocal cords. For the bed speaks. But it only speaks if you speak to it. As, in Grimm's fairy tales, all those dumb creatures, swans, trees hanging on every word, needing only to be addressed to find themselves once again children, sisters, brothers. If I'd only known I'd have asked my friend whether in his opinion the bed as reproducible object was just a bed without a soul or whether as bed owing its fate its solitude its misery its history to the thinker of "The Work of Art in the Age of Mechanical Reproduction" simultaneously with the German refugee ceaselessly dislodged dislodging with whom my mother had done business just before the poor lad set out for death, it might have inherited, in his opinion, an *auratic emanation*, despite its body flesh being metal. Is metal less apt to receive the signature, to emit the aura, than wood or cloth? I would so have liked to ask him. Another parergonic question: am I perhaps writing a book in order to ask my friend all these questions that I hadn't time to ask on the telephone?

In another chapter, it crosses my mind to try the bed. It's the first time. The bed is in the basement. I fall asleep faster than sleep so I go directly to dream without crossing the porch, I am sitting at my table therefore I cannot have left my desk right away I answer the phone that rang so fast I didn't pick up, I answer as fast, as if I'd guessed my friend was dialing my number and right away I hear his voice luckily my pen is poised to catch in flight whatever he tells me luckily with a few second thoughts and stutters that let me, if he goes too fast for the speed of my handwriting, catch up with a phrase and that give me a feel for the near distance from which he speaks to me so fast racing against time as one does when one fears being cut off without warning, which reminds me, even as I take notes, of what he used tell me about his telephone conversations with his friend Levinas forever trembling for fear the call would be cut off so that he would hang onto the phone anxiously repeating hello? hello? hello? as if the other person had been swept away by the long-distance powers before he on his end had had time to finish his sentence. I take notes and as I race along those slight stutters make me aware of the force of distance he must pierce to speak. I feel at each turn of the phrase that it describes a series of spirals as if to loop itself around his heart, I take notes shorthand, after a certain point his voice begins to trail off, I am terrified of waking before he comes to the end I freeze except at the wrist to be one with the music of this venerated voice not breathing a word or hello hello, for I know all too well the extreme frailty of what is granted, and how it depends on the state of interiority the hypnotized diver manages without breathing to maintain.

In the following transcription I keep everything, no way I'm going to lose a letter:

"*For we love best the things a book has first spoken to us of or someone whose words have the voice of someone who has for us the same authority as the thing written down in the first place spoke to us with. For then we. Before we saw it. Thus we can make it a* <u>*duplicate*</u> *of it* (here I underline because the voice underlined) *carry it in our hearts, warm it inside of us, dress it in all the ideas of* perfection you carry around inside of you, give it a *personality* (the voice underlines) and finally (and from this point it seemed to me the voice was going off but so eager was I to cling to it that my soul if not my body seemed to leap out of me so as to fling itself after the voice) to be eager to be in the presence of (this, *cette* or *cet*,) (here to my despair came a word I didn't catch and in despair I didn't stop myself however for then I should have missed what came next, the voice dimmed like the day but much too fast and still I wrote) – that we have endowed, *doué* (but should it perhaps be feminine: *douée*?) with so much *omnipotence other*" – and at these words, all the while writing faster than fast as if swept along by an omnipotence-other speed, I was thrilled to see my friend rapidly signaling to me in one of those gestures he was forever making, playful and childlike in the manner that was a convention of our friendship, which we called *making a citation* or sometimes *secretcitation.* We've never ceased, in the friendship I alone remain to speak of, seasoning the discourse of the one with words of the other, so naturally, so apparently spontaneously that no third person would ever detect a trace of soldering in the alloy of our phrases we the above signed and above all we undersigned. Him especially greatest of Citers was in the habit of sending me messages we between us called "Echoes," him batting back in my direction a few lines or syntagms that I'd once hit, that he'd been fastest in the whole world to receive as if he himself were just about to jot them down or had just that instant written the same himself, so that between us priority and simultaneity were mixed up, and as soon as he pronounced "omnipotence others" my heart shook as if standing on a train platform, eyes straining in the direction of the train that blurs the traveler I caught the flicker of a handkerchief way off at the other end of the image. A handkerchief! Yet another scrap of the soul's fabric that is vanishing from the Farewell Scenes. I thought all that in the same breath as that which carried the final words of the sentence, I was thinking, I was jotting, I was reliving I was receiving I was laughing I was losing I was finding again, I was grasping the phrase, the voice, the absolute, *in duplicate*, everything was double; this instant, and its past doubled up, a double of this instant and its future double; this dictation and its future double; this dream and its double, which would remain; the reality of this dream in the dream the reality of this dream out of the dream; this scene took me from happiness to unhappiness, and in admiration I dreamed the dream and its double, *in* the dream, following the directions in the voice of my friend, I understood he was reminding me to make a copy, a duplicate to carry in our hearts the sentence was saying, then as in a dream I came to the turn of breath where I saw the voice fade just in time to throw on paper *that our eyes if only we keep them focused on her could not have transmitted*, words thank heavens I managed to hear twice for I could not write them down until my friend's voice had gone on its way, but I had them by heart even if I hadn't caught their meaning for lack of the presence of mind. I on my side was nothing but a heart. Still, I hadn't an ounce of doubt that on his side wisdom and sense were secure, watched out for, kept safe, and that they would be waiting for me whenever I wished to come back to the thing a second time. I was in a rush to wake up in the dream. I mean: in the dream I was in a rush to wake up anxious to check on the state of the inscriptions. Because I knew I was in a dream doubtless caused by the auratic force of the bed. I had confidence in the bed and in all the powers that had inhabited it for such a long time, in Benjamin's and J.D.'s marvelous and full-of-authority spirits that shaped a heart for its carcass, so long abandoned so far from any civilization. I didn't doubt the dream. I trembled that turning a light on in the dream to consult the manuscript might waken some Forgetfulness that would gulp down my treasure. Or to find myself on the bed as on the straw, as the narrator of *Sodom and Gomorrah* holds to his heart a fork whose formula he has lost and which however aboard the dream that is now disembarking him had alchemical omnipotence. The danger always awaits us at the exit. I lit so little. Everything – everything was lying there – in big gauche ugly round readable letters – dropped syllable by syllable – all was scattered chopped up but readable like a shy duplicate.

Right away I develop a flame for the bed. I can feel myself loving it for each of the powers fate has endowed it with: history, philosophy, neurosis, friendship, chagrin, the ideas of immortality, the genius of dreaming, the mystery of the resurrection, the resistance to being reduced to nothing. I would go so far as to make a copy of it in my heart, give it a personality that speaks German and French. I wouldn't dream of abusing the bed. That its power has given me so much this time isn't eternally binding.

– Do you know what the subject of your book is? says my brother. "It looks with anguish into the abyss of the coming months," like Benjamin on June 5, 1937 my book and I look into the abyss and see only the anguish of the months ahead, a person I say can't know what lies ahead, he catches the intoxicating peppery scent of the final last times, he thinks about moving, it has to do with the move to the kingdom of death, I say – I repeat what I see writing itself in the abyss – the abyss begins just under the windows, with each move one loses a little being and a lot of time, people were always coming and going says Mummy, she calls them "the repatriated," this is an error says my brother, it's summative I say, the refugees leave a refuge, enter a refuge run to the windows, what they see makes them move on they move, refuge means move, move moves on into madness, my book I say is on the move, we are moving each other

I suppose that in the eyes of the generations to come, we'll appear as twisted by our mortal and mental maladies as Benjamin's generation could without difficulty and with anguish imagine itself appearing to the next generation that is to say ours, dragging around after ourselves a mixed bag of ghosts, refugees and survivors of wounds to the heart

On July 9, 1937 he wonders if there mightn't be a sort of historico-cosmic year during which demons are let loose.

Upon his return from the no-refuge, having found his old room under foreign occupation as a result of some unforeseeable machination on the part of his hostess of the previous day, he has no choice but to move. It's his fifth move since the bed. *One can always lose more.* During the final last times one makes some rare finds whose influence on the work is said to be decisive, everything happens as if fate were in a hurry to grant us some of the rare loss to come. First of all Benjamin happens in extremis on the text *the last, written by Blanqui in the last of his prisons*, Fort Taureau. It is called *Eternity by the Stars.* Next I happen on Benjamin's letter that has fallen just before the final straw onto Blanqui's last text. To reach Eternity via the stars you need to be on the move for the last time –

Your book is on that Benjamin? says my brother. – On the moves of the stars I say, on the chinks in the walls of the last refuge, on the state of the wallpaper

– Strange, says my brother. I wish I understood.

The strangeness increases. The weight of the strangeness. The weights

The armchair cracks, and that's an end of it. End of the armchair. It's the chair, says my brother. Such an old chair. It's *fichu* done for. We discuss the cause of the end of the armchair coeval of the bed. Twenty-buck chair says my brother. For me it's irreplaceable. In my opinion this armchair might have survived another six months, a year even. It's a problem keeping the chair, with its crack. Everything that's done for you cling to, I wish I understood. That bench downstairs, a piece of junk. The bench from the Clos-Salembier, a monumental piece of junk. Preserving it is problematic for me. The wood is full of worms. My idea is we'll lay a board across it, says my mother. A shame to throw it out. You never know who might sit down on it. A good for ghosts bench. My brother would really like to understand. Are you constructing? What am I doing? When

I start asking myself what I'm doing there's only one reason: because my brother puts the screws on. For one thing I'm looking after my mother's skin, that is, my own chances of survival. I add: anointing my mother I anoint Time, Memory, the Century, everything she doesn't know I caress. I chase away the crevasses. – One shouldn't use cortisone in such high doses says my brother, it weakens us, it's dangerous for Mummy. One cannot not use the cortisone, one must weaken Mummy to keep her alive so as to weaken her, weaken life to hold onto life, I run to all the windows everywhere the weather looks threatening and I gaze with anguish into the abyss of the months ahead. If I don't weaken my mother a swarm of sores like demons will squeeze through all the cracks and folds and the mouth even and the throat even. "One can always lose differently" I tell my brother – there's what anguishes my book, but right away I regret these words. Everything one says renders the subject more fragile.

Maybe it's time I'm at work on, I tell myself. I have my brother by the waist. All of a sudden I plant a kiss on his cheek: all of a sudden his cheek comes to kiss my lips. He is tiny. His name is Pierre. I hadn't thought that before. I am astounded at the idea that after all his skin his ear are parts of his father, therefore come from my father. I hadn't thought that before. Suddenly my father is in my brother. *Mon pére est dans mon frère.* Time is our subject, I tell myself. Time is a mystery. At work on what is invisible to us, what doesn't exist, what comes right up and kisses us. We make time we watch over it. My father is all around us here. My friend is in the air, I breathe him. I feel very strongly the presence of all Time the invisible around us. My brother and I together carry the Moses basket of time. I am as moved as on the day of burial we weren't with my father, he lost us in the cemetery, we were losing our father separately each on our own side.

– I am painting Mummy, I say.

When I paint my mother, I paint the skin of the century. This twentieth century so big viewed from afar, so small viewed from within when one is so packed into one's train one must go looking for somewhere to sleep on hands and knees and which hasn't for an instant stopped making my mother's history. Each time a sore scars another one takes the pus's place. One can't get over it. One runs after the illness. One changes sores. I myself grow accustomed to looking at the put-out eyes I look at them from behind a visor of tears. There are more and more of them.

– "You are time" I say.

– What have you got against time? asks my mother. I myself throw nothing away. Time is when you've nothing to do and you attempt to shift the gun to the other shoulder. At my age so far I've never wanted to kill time. It's a pity to waste it.

Thatremindsme of three men. I was in an office three of them propositioning me. One had just married. This was of no interest whatsoever to me. An older one said: there's no risk, I won't get you pregnant. Tell that to the next one I said. Do you know that expression? The third the boss who'd invited me to a good restaurant told me I could give you a studio, some pieces of jewelry. This was not of the slightest interest to me. The meal was very good. Jewels no. Furs no. The other had a troupe of *girls* in Berlin. You've got breasts that aren't going to sag, I am an expert, in Berlin I had *girls*. He hadn't seen her naked. All these folks dead and gone. When I look at myself in the nude – I see my breasts are still in good shape. I don't let myself go. I always remember those bosses I had, Berlin bosses, nice bosses I had Alsatians Protestants not anti-Jews. All those dead and gone people I remember so well.

Legs straight, speckled, titties proud as in the old days I dab and I coat the wide apart little breasts which today are still in good shape

I fear losing two centuries, the century that is my mother and the century that I'm going to have to get by with no friend and no Mummy.

But July 15 just at noon, the man who pitched his tent in the crocodile's jaw propped open with iron bars, called Benjamin, receives birthday wishes with joy. That day he's preparing to move a hundred or so books into a wretched pied-à-terre. All he has is a room at ground level along one of the main roads out of Paris, where he will be assaulted by lorry din on all sides. They call that *un* pied-à-terre – *one* foot on the ground – the other's already in the grave he writes

I had been waiting for this July 15 which would be back to roll its birthday wheel over my heart, its archi-mythic wheel, the din in the kitchen is my mother with hammer and knife, attacking a fish, she pounds and pounds, it's July 15 I shout, I was sure she'd have forgotten, you forgot the date I shouted over the din of hammer on knife, you need to eat fish my mother shouts, I ask no one in this house for help, then she gets on the phone hand still the color of the fish's execution, and continues trumpeting about no one in the house to slaughter a fish with a hammer dead as alive, one has no idea what strength resisting death gives. My mother with her sick sister on her mind, they give one another advice about their two illnesses illnesses, shouting sisters, sister deafness, hammer knife fish between two kitchens, their co-deafness calls out knife hammer fish crocodile, they're tuning their springs, they co-will their bodies to one another sometimes they toss one another instructions in French thought to be English sometimes my mother shouts English in German, the language of languages chopped up fine and hauled in, speak English I say, it's better for your sister over in England, what am I saying, she doesn't care *elle s'en fiche* shouts my mother, *fish* calls my aunt in Manchester, dried cod *wie heisst das* here? on the tips of their several tongues quick quick they pass the body parts back and forth between them my aunt's teeth dropped *on the floor*, the two cancers both have left in their wake, they've had their cancers and they've forgotten them

suddenly I weep, between two floors, quick, the future memory strikes me hammer knife my life in pieces I'll remember I had a quick cry unable either to live or to die only keep going how happy I was then I'll tell myself, I still had my mother to lose on the telephone with my aunt

Time is full of bodies and medicines

The dialogues go on about bones about ears about tummy upsets, *implants* cries my mother, French has won out. *Implants!* You don't know that? my mother gives a whoop of victory.

She's slaughtering the fish, I say – You didn't see her buy it, says my brother. She doesn't buy anything without an umbrella. Not that one. With her umbrella she points at the other one. She doesn't talk. Doesn't answer. Points her umbrella. That one. In the old days I'd never have stood for it. With her umbrella she points at the radishes. Not that. That! Later we'll walk along the border, paradise will be hell, hell skirts paradise I tell myself and vice versa, I'm walking with my brother and all my dead at my side, I feel my skeleton decalcifying within the appearance of my body, my brother's skeleton slows down, you don't know how to take your time says my brother, I don't know anything I say I'm rushing from yet to never again.

On the way out on July 15 if I get ahead I come back, we'll go to the blockhouse says my brother we'll go to the Blockhouse I say, Blockhouse, the name of the unknown soldiers, all those Germans, they would shoot through the loopholes, all those soldiers have now been changed into regiments of mussels, thousands of scaly helmets, war is metal dust, from the blockhouse we'll turn back I say, I write from the Blockhouse, from the total oblivion of a vestige of dread and despair, a concrete skull whose frightened orbits the ocean and the wind will have the time of times to chew over.

On the way: tender Mummy, I wish I understood, she's always rejected me, sixty years of being rejected, suddenly she turns all tender, says my brother, what's your take on that? You're in a rush? I'm in more and more of a rush, my brother the complete opposite. I see Sero coming up, I tell myself. Emperor of the infernal times. My brother talks I listen telling myself "I'll be telling myself." It'll be a July 15. The thought of that invisible July 15 casts over this one a transparent and glacial shadow. On the way, charming Mummy, she called me "my son" says my brother, for sixty-five years one waits, one expects nothing, it bothers me she should call me "my son" now I am moved, it'd upset me if she were to stop. Do you know Sero? I say. – Who's that? – I'll tell you later. – You are making my mouth water. I walk once around the Blockhouse, blockhouse of the Homerless, the unsung tortured, a tomb now exhumed now buried a wretched reservoir of the dead, urn. Unvisited. Concrete record. An abstract pity, universal, borderless, paperless takes me out and brings me back. A grave can die too I tell myself. "I am furnished with dying tombs," I was thinking. Yet another thought to dig under the radishes and the strawberries.

"As long as she is alive, I tell myself, I haven't yet lost anything of all that I have lost."

This sentence makes me want to hurry back and check up on Mummy. I go on living on the idea that I continue to live on the life of my mother. On my mother's conception of life. I think tomb. She thinks: strawberries. One will see my mother coming back from the market where despite the increasing frailty of her body, fragility of her bones, loss of her independence and mobility, despite the loss of vigor and speed imposed upon her by the person who only accompanies her in order to keep her on her leash, but in vain, eyes sparkling, one will no longer see the wizened little face with its spotty crinkly tissues, only the superhuman brightness of the eyes in their glory enlarged, in a state of transfiguration in which I suddenly recognize, as if she'd come back to me in a dream, the essence and secret of her grandeur, the example not two meters away from me of the immensity of life for life's sake, the radiant all-powerfulness of the principle of being and having what one is and what one has, without letting anything wound one. You will see my mother proclaim from afar: "We found what you need!" And me, not knowing what I need. "Strawberries!" And I, I shall not tell her that day that *Strawberries* were really and truly and conditionally what I needed. The condition is the miraculous fishing trip, and my mother is the fisher.

De profundis we found *what you need.* Strawberries. And a chamber pot for her sister.

– She's getting easier and easier to put up with, says my brother. That cortisone dries up the skin, toughens it, I don't see any weals, when I bend my great stiff carcass down to her she tips up her chin and she smiles. Strange. I wish I understood. Says my brother on July 15. We are walking on the border of sky and earth we are walking along time, along July 15 before the sun comes up again the sand washed by the ocean, we were walking at different speeds, each responds in a different manner to the emperor's message, me hurrying my brother ambling, I shall think, I had just entered trembling into the time of the final last times I will tell myself, the dread spring of the last times was in its dread greenness, I'll be thinking, who knows what color the sorrow will be when I see my brother and me walking side by side across the earth on that July 15 which will come out of the past and walk onto the stage, I will be facing us, and at the same time I'll be on the path again beside my brother, me shut up behind the door my brother wide open, I tell myself, I don't know whether I'll devour my own heart or if I'll fall down dead like a cadaver or if I will want to have enough strength to taste the misfortune my mother will have bequeathed me, along with the umbrella

that's what I tell myself walking faster and faster coming back from the walk on the dune, my brother puts the brakes on, but ever since the Blockhouse I've been accelerating, as if a quick return might stave off fatality. I flee beneath the idea of the end, I accuse myself of being unreasonable, I am in the crocodile's jaws and I have nothing to prop them open, furthermore this summer is the first summer in my history and the first summer in my work when the possibility of telephone between my friend and me has become impossibility of telephone, an impossibility whose force is preserved in the memories of mobiles and telephones that display first the name of my friend and his telephone number before they tirelessly announce that the number I am calling is no longer in service. Over and over the female voice says this number is no longer in service and one doesn't believe it.

Nor can I telephone my mother, I can't risk my mother not answering, instead of my mother, deafness, I don't telephone my mother I'm too frightened she won't answer, telephone her and not have her answer plunges me into the depths of despair, not telephone her is on the one hand a matter of thrift, on the other hand it stops me from putting out the fire,

I can't make my brother hurry up 1) it's impossible 2) I admit that my brother also has rights 3) I can't tell my brother

I'm afraid Mummy will disappear, one has a perfect right to fail in one's duty but this a private right 4) I have no objective reason on that day to fear Mummy may disappear, my objective, imaginary, subjective, superstitious reasons are only too plentiful, I can't overcome them, I succumb to the weight of July 15, nothing however tells me that my mother is not at this very moment in danger, she has slipped, she has fallen, or perhaps she is sitting on her bed laughing herself to tears with Monsieur Pons, the name of that fool of a Cousin Pons, with whom she's been holed up ever since I gave her Balzac's book last week. These days there are three characters to be reckoned with in my mother's room: Deafness, the Umbrella and Monsieur Pons. In the struggle for life each of them is sometimes on the right side sometimes on the wrong.

We are coming back. My brother is speaking. I look at my watch. She's started shouting at me again. Going out she is tender. Coming back she won't stop grumbling, here are a few examples. "The apple!" shouts my brother. He shouts: the apple! He is doing my mother. He shouts her. The apple! Splats in the forest. Why don't you wash the apple? Mummy! Do you treat your daughter like that? I'll give you an example. I take her to the fish market. Mummy bellows. Take this road! shouts my brother. Unless I want to be squashed I take that road. She shouts: Take the other. With her umbrella. She shouts. The other! he shouts. She points at the other as if she took herself for Napoleon. If she's not wrong she squashes you. For a whole hour. For years. With the umbrella! Everything is less and less bearable. Just when I'm about to tell her let's not take this road the other is shorter. He brandishes my mother's umbrella, he shouts: the other! I wish I understood says my brother. On the way out I say we're going away from her. On the way back we're going towards her. Just as I'm hearing myself say these sentences, I tip over. My entire being doubles up. I stop a second to take my shoes off. Sand in my sandal, I say. But in truth it's my thinking that is lame. I don't know what it or *elle* is about. I don't know to whom *she* refers. I bend down, leaning on my brother. That way my tears don't run down me, they drip into the sand.

It makes you think one dies too fast.

The weather turns threatening. For forty years we thought of death of life of death of death of life after that of death then of life, after death of death after death of life of the going away then of the coming back, we get away from it, the further away we get the closer we are we run to every window for forty years the same storm, each time we get away from it we think of death, we are giving life to death, I would say we're putting death to death my friend would say, let's not talk about it he would say, we're giving life to death, each time we talk about it let's not talk about it any more my friend would say, we don't talk about it any more.

We don't talk about it any more. I think about it all the time. Everything I say everything I think runs along this road narrow as the crest of a dune, we slither from side to side, we don't talk about it any more, the minute you think you're not talking about it any more you think more and more about not thinking about it and we have to start all over again J.D. would say may we always have to begin again he'd say, first go, not so fast, go further more slowly, slow down, I'm always behind, he would say, I'm always having to call you back, to remind you of death he would say, in the end I'm always having to remind you that on my side we die too fast, while you on your side live too fast, he would tell me, you don't recall, up to three times a week, he would call me up to remind me, you don't believe me, you know, and don't see, he used to say into the phone, he called me back he sent his voice out into the dark, you don't recall he would say, no no I would say, I don't recall up to two or three times, over the years

I was walking in the forest alongside my brother he has a perfect right to go so slowly, I was in a rush to get back to my mother, the forest was gradually turning into future cemetery, the world is completely different I was thinking, I was fleeing but one doesn't know which meaning, which direction of fleeing, time flies, I flee time, go, come back I am still with my brother I told myself, without knowing really what this phrase meant nor what I meant either, besides am I with my brother at his side, or am I meanwhile or on the contrary with my friend whose voice I heard inside me telephoning "not all that long ago my friend on the telephone" I was saying it wasn't long ago but since one particular date "not long ago" is something utterly changed, it's as if I said 1940 and it's a garden whose gates have been shut in our faces, this new world with its forests as hollow as the cheeks of hundred-year-olds is beyond him

time having gone full circle, the present seemed past to me, even as I was walking towards my mother with my brother not knowing what would happen when I took up the argument with my inner friend again

over the years, I tell myself, I ended up surrendering completely to the strange evidence of the essence of our friendship. We never stop talking of stopping and starting, stopping beginning starting up again without ever stopping starting to finish as late as possible, of his craft and his art of my craft and my art whose subject according to me is living and in the end you die – and according to my friend it is thinking living and thinking of the end and thinking in the end one dies, too fast and thinking the too-fast doing all one can to slow down thinking what the too fast implies. Such was the theme of all our times and for years

this thinking "that one dies too fast" which makes us live and think, too fast I told myself too fast perhaps to be able to ask myself in the bottom of my soul what I could do about this *too fast* that my friend would say over and over in the end I reminded myself we'd forever be having to start all over again him telling me on the phone remember, on my side one dies, in the end, too fast, me on my side telling him I don't think so, are you sure? do you recall, yes I recall I don't believe it, over the years I was starting to start to believe that I really didn't believe that in the end, one dies, too fast, on his side, the years pleaded, my friend pleaded, every time he called finally I saw that he was pleading against what he believed, he reached out with his voice to touch my voice so as to reassure himself it wasn't trembling when I said I don't think so, I began to understand that I would always be having to start over not believing what I knew, the main thing is not knowing it is knowing not to believe it, I'd ended up thinking that the closer one got the less one needed to believe the more I'd have to remind myself not to believe, over time I'd come to wonder if he wanted to call me back to his side or did he want me to call him back to my side, that is to the side where he believed I didn't believe that in the end one dies, too fast, calling me two or three times in succession to remind me that I on my side still didn't believe whereas he on his side believed too quickly, that in the end one dies, whereupon believing that I saw that my friend did not want to convince me but on the contrary to convince himself he hadn't convinced me, in spite of his unstinting efforts to remind me that on his side, one dies too fast and despite the great authority he always exercised over me, and above all despite his constant wielding of this authority, having begun to think over time that my friend was once again making sure that he hadn't been able to shake my conviction, despite not having spared his saliva, his anxiety, his authority, going so far as to call me fifty or more times each year on the topic of his wretched belief and my stubborn contrariness

and this despite the fact that, contrary to what my friend believed I believed, I'd always been racked by fear, anguish, apprehension, despite my having had to struggle my whole life long against the malediction that strikes me the instant I love, casting an aura of fatality over any person I have the good fortune therefore worse luck to love, despite me in my view having always known – which my friend knew – starting with the brutal and catastrophic death of my father therefore from the age of ten, that too soon the hour of separation comes, and having already lived through death more than once I have never been for life save against death, having always known, I have never therefore been able to do otherwise, for the simple sake of survival, than be content to live from life to life day to day, astonishment to astonishment, finding life so much longer than what death gave me to think from the very first dawn, I was always having to start all over finding life longer than expected so as not to die of fear several times each week, and because if I started knowing what I know and believing what I believe I'd have already crossed to the other side, that is to the side of my friend, that is I'd have passed on, ages ago

by dint of reminding myself that life is longer than I believe it to be on my side whereas he on his side was forever calling me to the phone to remind me what he on his side thought: one dies in the end too fast, in the end I'd started to believe I might believe what I on my side was supposed to believe, so that on his side he might believe what he couldn't keep from believing and what he couldn't believe without putting his powers of reason and perhaps even his life at risk and being sure that I on my side believed the contrary, however, that which on my side had come to constitute, in the long run, by dint of beginning and re-beginning our singular dispute on the telephone, a choice of sorts, mandated by the violent pressure of circumstances, hence a decision but taken who knows when who knows at what depth, in which murmurous back corner of the mind, to stick to a belief the opposite of his, this was never so simple, in one way it allowed him to tell himself:

"if only I might believe her" or "oh! if I could only believe her, if . . ." with the result that this slender if was like a wire to which he could cling in order to drift on the tenebrous tide of his belief that death in the end comes too fast, putting some minimal limit to the risk of drowning; but on the other hand I was thinking if he tells himself I'm right and he's wrong, he is allowing himself to drift on the black tide of his unreason. However in the end this debate had for me an unforeseen consequence: over time it became impossible for me to express the least un-steadfastness of conviction without putting the whole lifeboat in danger, along with its frail and meticulous arrangements, which made it impossible for me to let myself be shaken either by myself or by him and hence to risk expressing the least shadow of a doubt without wreaking incalculable havoc.

Eventually, at first by dint of thinking I didn't for a moment believe what he kept reminding me of: "one dies in the end, too fast" at first on the telephone, one or more times a week for years (which goes to prove the struggle, the difficulty, the necessity) then in writing – as if it were necessary to add to prophetic speech the gravity, the authority that paper's publicity confers upon the word – as if he took the world as witness to our two faiths, the in good faith and bad, and by dint of tracing magic circles in time at whose center the dispute might start up again, I took to imitating faith in this not-believing what he had transformed into a lesson of thought then into a philosophy. In the beginning I imitated it out of the discreet computation dictated by tenderness and respect, so as to limit the anguish, even using a subterfuge, such as friendship requires, during the first ten or fifteen years I countered the assault of those few words, so terrifying so terrified so authoritative so anxious to be contradicted and de-authorized but one must not say or do so, with responses that were frankly neither here nor there, modulated by a "not always," a "save exceptions" an "except in your case," I first took a step towards him, then the following moment I backed off, I made a credible show of faith which is to say firm but shakable but victorious over doubt, in which in the beginning I myself in my heart of hearts did not for a second believe but which seemed nonetheless not totally lacking in sense. So that, had I not myself been already so wounded and terrified I might almost in truth have believed this. Therefore I wasn't lying. I was doing my job. I wavered but only in secret. And I had the fortitude as champion of the king of death to seem rebellious in the face of his speech. But fortitude to seem is already fortitude to be and this fortitude to have the fortitude to seem I had. What gave it me, I must say, was him, that is it was the solicitude which his need to be at one and the same time approved and contradicted naturally aroused in the camp of friendship as a force good for him inasmuch as it joined with his own life forces against his own death forces. Nonetheless the equilibrium of the measure had each and every time to be recalibrated, for to muster up too much resistance to his forces of death would naturally have merely reinforced them. I compromised. For years at every phone call I adjusted, I tossed in a pinch of light or semi-dark pragmatically, letting myself be guided by the thickness, the variation of rhythm, of the slowness-speed of the timbre of the brightness and vice versa of his second voice as highly precise indicator of the state of his soul. Naturally I trusted to his second voice in my supersensitive groping, the way you tune a musical instrument better with your eyes closed, for years, I never stopped tuning I mean tuning *and* un-tuning several times a month the tone and tension of the arguments I tossed into the dispute relying on hints I noted at top speed, on the spot, as soon as I detected the first notes of the second voice, the telephone voice. The same thing in person at the same moment in the same room, study, living room, would have been another body of voices, would have been the voice with hands, the voice clothed. But always I let myself be guided by the voice he called "defenseless," the second, the voice to which distance allows repose and disarmament. "Between voices you hear each other better than when you see each other." *Entre voix on s'entend mieux que lorsque l'on se voit*. Montaigne was right. Just as Montaigne and La Boetie telephoned one another, without which they wouldn't have reached so absolutely and simultaneously the heart of hearts and all the knots and ties, later designated by the vocables beginning with co-, would never have existed. The telephone was installed in the Tower between the first little room the one with the starry sky, on whose wall St George small on his horse is painted in the likeness of La Boetie coming at a gallop to the call of Montaigne who is in the box hollowed out of the stone one floor up, where for ease of conversation – for the phone box is narrow – they set a chair as small as a prie-dieu. The acoustics are excellent. Stone carries. Let your heart murmur, the other hears perfectly. The décor of the two scenes in which the call takes place means that wherever you may be in heaven or under the heavens the other on earth or underneath the suit of armor, neither iron nor stone will ever interrupt the connection. To be together without either losing his solitude, to remain alone each on his or her side without the whole breaking, this is what the miracle contrives.

The whole time I worked for him, I had to work against him, I worked against him for his sake, I did his job, which job I don't know, when it was necessary to disobey I obeyed: I disobeyed. At the moment of disobeying I obeyed. I see clearly that I let myself be guided by his second voice down the path where he was waiting for me to guide him, but without hope, right to his front door. Thus: I followed on his heels a fraction of a second behind I carried out the order so fast it was as if I went on ahead, so that when he rang, I would be there to let him in.

This is neither impossible nor unique, even if it is both unique and impossible. I receive the SOSs of my cats before the messages are sent and vice versa. I write this sentence, you will have noticed, as he would have written it and as he wrote it in other words

Today I recall only the broad outlines of this work that knew no rest, forever on its way without a terminus airborne without a runway, journeying without arriving right up to the day I heard myself say loud and clear on the phone, in a rapid, firm voice, that I for my part did not in the least believe that on his side "one dies in the end, too fast." That was early in the 90s. I could find the date in my notebooks. Suddenly the evidence was blinding. Suddenly I saw that I truly didn't believe what he wanted me to believe and also wanted me not to believe. As if *I had begged the question* and it had been granted me. Now I really was on my team, on my side. I had won myself over, I'd won over my father's daughter inside of me. That day I felt the invincible little body of my mother quicken inside me. I might have expected a little of the German scratchiness of my mother's voice to mix with my voice. Luckily this didn't happen. Being on my side just as my friend had always imagined and thought, I naturally and effortlessly became his ally against himself on his side therefore against his own deadly forces. Now I had my mother inside me just as she keeps inside her, and not just on her wrist, her umbrella.

He was getting going again. "And it's starting up again. And it's starting up again." I quote him. His version of the endless dispute was published once in 1998 and then again in 2002 and in 2003. *And it's starting up again* was him. *And it's starting up again* was me. Twice.

"Me, he would say to whoever cared to listen, I'm each and every time reminding her that on my side, one dies in the end, too fast." Adding: "I'm always having to start over again." You should have heard him. You would have to hear him, him, and the sentence as well. "Me" he would say, and he points to me – *lui* – with his voice, on my side of the sentence I am "*lui*." Me, as you are my witness, he would say, first with one voice then another voice and next he wrote it and he has written and published it in a book, which gave at the time and henceforth gives who knows what weight to the declaration that he reread and signed and in which he addresses a group of people, an audience, the public, so as to inform them of the existence of the *interminable dispute* he calls it and give them an idea of the singular nature of the dispute, that is give to whoever wants to hear it his version and feeling on the subject of that extraordinary dispute. In June 1998 *for the first time* I hear him (the first voice) give an assembly, of which I was part, an overview and résumé of the "dispute" that had been going on for several decades and which I learned at that point for the first time was called a "dispute," *a singular dispute*, he said and what's more read, because he had written this text in April and May 1998, and he was speaking reading and rereading what he had already written read reread and reread on his side and therefore in all likelihood thought some weeks earlier. Singular and what's more: *all but interminable*. And that was him to a T, "that's him to a T" I tell myself, without knowing at that moment how I could, if someone challenged me on the spot, account grammatically, philosophically for my categorical deep conviction that I was justified in thinking "that's him to a T," when I don't know what *that's* means, nor *to a T*, nor him, who him. Probably I couldn't have. Even to myself I could not explain how this shook me. I was KO. As if the telephone rang and froze me on the spot.

I was sitting in the second row of the assembly hall. It seemed to me I discerned in this long sentence, which wasn't addressed to me, a note of complaint against "*lui*" that is me and against "*elle*" that is me, or maybe I believed I discerned or maybe I feared I should believe I heard a sigh, a note of lassitude, in this long sentence which must, in order to address itself to me, not be addressed to me, but to her-*elle*, to her-*lui* who he is always reminding in vain "that one dies in the end, too fast," a note of lassitude at the idea that he on his side always has to start up again, reminding me that on his side, one dies in the end, too fast, and therefore "she-*elle*" is each and every time again starting to-not-believe-a-word-of-it, but right away I plugged my ears, and even somehow ceased to be sitting in the assembly hall. There's a blank there.

We are back. Mummy is asleep. It is 9:30 a.m. I listen at the door. Not a peep. I go upstairs to my study. I look at the trees. The two squirrels are spiraling around the oak. I go downstairs. It is 10 o'clock. Mummy is asleep. I go in. She is on her side. Only the small face that was once normal-sized today all shrunken the rest tucked under the quilt. Mouth agape. I go over. I touch the cheek. It is warm. I go out, I close the door. Mummy is asleep. Nobody to tell: worried, I touched my mother's cheek. She is still sleeping. Give me faith, diminished Goddess.

At the door, the umbrella keeps watch. I see the umbrella. A new being in the house. It is an extra-large umbrella, not your usual umbrella but a cane acting the part of an umbrella. Its ballooning sails lend it a certain modesty. The new one. Hard-nosed specter. My mother's companion and scepter. My brother and I haven't come up with a nickname for it. She waves the umbrella and the extent of her dominion doubles. She raises her rod and stammerers speak. Shopkeepers are most impressed. Shopkeepers are very nice with the umbrella my brother says. The whole world speaks in signs. This rapid silence that the umbrella spreads around it scares me. According to my brother all of my mother's authority is vested in the umbrella. In my opinion my mother gave herself up to the umbrella after years of being besieged. My mother's body will go away. The umbrella will remain. I will have to keep and protect it to the end. I may become attached to it. I will be its dog perhaps. Or it mine. One day perhaps I will be passionately unwilling to let go of the umbrella that today I regard with hostility. I may not be able to get along without this vestige of Mummy. I'll have forgotten my reproach of today July 15, which I am writing in my notebook.

I'm coming back many years later to *the sentence* uttered by my friend in June 1998. This was in March 2005, as I wrote on the book itself, I was in the train. I never read in the train. It would not have been impossible for me to have read that sentence much earlier, objectively speaking, I could have read it on the proofs, it was published in 2000, then again in 2002. I note. Hence I was unable to have done otherwise. I couldn't read it. Until the day when I couldn't not want to read it. I could no longer put it off. I read it in the train, I who am incapable of reading anything on the high-speed train.

This sentence is now stretched out across the bottom of page 9 of *H.C pour la vie c'est à dire. . .*

I take it. I put it on the loom. I spread it out. It is a body where from one angle the veins the muscles, the tendons appear, from another the skin. I can hear it breathe, hesitate, fall silent. Read it over from the beginning and it's something else. There's what he says and what she says, and there's what he writes, and there's what what he writes doesn't say and nonetheless says. It's all in the commas, all the power, the true, the false the flight, the anger, the salvation, the incredulity, the unbelievability: commas.

I finger it. It twists between my paws, it puts its commas out: Me, *(comma)*

I am each and every time having to remind her, *(comma)* on my side, *(comma)*

one dies in the end, *(comma)*

too fast.

Too fast shakes off the comma. No comma! Fast!

I observe his weaving. It begins with me already. *Me*, each time he says *me*, it's a way to say *not-her*, hence *her*, not-me:

her, not her: me. The sentence swings back and forth, from him to her. He throws me off. He says he's the one I set swinging, I push him to throw me off, he denounces his own inability, which is mine, to stop swinging from believe to believe, he denounces me for not being able to keep him from swinging, I hunch my shoulders, I tuck in my chin.

Then he throws out everything he seems to have said he was saying, with one comma he throws away everything he says he thought

Moreover he says *too fast* so in the end one has no idea what in the end he thought of what he was in the act of saying, of writing, of reading

Was what he wanted to say that one always dies in the end and that if one says so, if one feels the need to say what the whole world believes it knows I tell myself, it's that this is not true, not really, maybe one doesn't always die in the end, maybe one dies before, maybe one dies as soon as one utters the dies, the die word, at least "on his side"

That one dies in the end, I tell myself, who could deny, but *what else* did he want to say I say to myself, for if he says this, that one dies in the end, it's that this is not true, this is not what he is saying, I know him a little, could I forget what I know? and now the whole world will know what I always forget, this is a grave and frightening thing, to die is what

it's as if I had to go back home on foot, alone, barefoot not knowing where far away, everybody else went long ago and I'm the barefoot remains of the congregation in shoes

And here beside me is a courteous person an attentive young man who shows me a tiny picture shot from another planet, one sees the gods in white loincloths plunging into a Ganges, which seems to be at the end of the world, isn't that my friend stepping into the mother stream? Do you recognize him? I lean in. It is so far away. I ask for a magnifying glass to no avail. I don't think it can be him. Don't you recognize him? An astonished murmur bends the branches of the assembly

as if everyone else knows what I've never heard of.

But on the other hand if I reel in the sentence again, starting with *too fast*, who says that he's not himself the Me, who acknowledges being in a rush to remind her – me in other words – of that which I have not in the least forgotten?

Slow down, I tell myself. This sentence twists and turns, nimble, between my teeth on my tongue, squirms out of my grip and darts off too fast for me to keep more than a tiny snippet of lizard tail.

I wonder I say to myself if this sentence didn't get away from him so fast that he needs to try to recapture its lightning flash.

I wonder to no avail if he himself had all his ears and teeth when the sentence struck his tongue

There's what he says, there's what it – the sentence – says, there's what is said, there's what is said about it, what we say about it, *always-notalways*, *each time having to in the end*, *too fast*, and each and every time there's what is said and what we say about it depending on whether one adds a modalization, or two, or all of them all together to each of the segments trapped between the comma-paws.

It's as if his writing didn't believe in what it was saying. It's as if he didn't believe the door would open, an unbelieving riddled with commas. It's as if he took me for a comma which he'd be well advised to put faith in but that a flick of the thumb would suffice to get rid of

It's as if his writing didn't believe what I've been telling him for decades, but him yes, a little, all the same.

– Everything depends on the *too fast.*

Since I *read* this sentence, a few months ago, I've been wondering, *too fast*, does *too fast* mean *too fast* or *too soon?* I don't believe one dies quickly, I believe one dielives. I should have told him, I tell myself, I believe one dies extremely slowly all the time and that's life, I believe that one livediescomma – and the full stop? I think he would have said to me: and the full stop, what do you make of that?

I should have asked him. I tell myself. "Now, I think about wanting to ask him what this too-fast that I really don't understand is all about," I think, "now I think about it" I tell myself and it's this now-that-I-to-no-avail-wish-I-could-ask-him-a-question which reminds me that one dies in the end, little by little one catches death while continuing to live.

I ought to have asked him.

I wonder why I didn't.

It makes me ill. I have dreams about this.

Maybe in the end it's all about starting over I tell myself. Perhaps it's all hidden in the "And I'm always having to start again," hidden or in full view, on that day in June 1998 when he spoke these sentences, in his voice there would have been some hint of affect, one can say the words of starting again with lassitude, irritation, exasperation, or with wonder, relief, exultation, with patience or serenity. I don't recall. I swing this way and that. Then I lean towards the hypothesis of a desire to start over, even if this meant starting over to remind oneself in the end, just as sometimes impatience may hold a jot of paradoxical pleasure.

"I wonder why I didn't ask him. I wonder *sero* why I wonder too late why I didn't ask during all those years. I wanted him to be right and I didn't know this."

I write this in a long notebook I started in November 2003. The cover reproduces the Serpent Painting from the *Livre de la Thériaque*. This is the notebook in which I file wild beasts, bites and stings, serpents, electuaries. Snakes slither up and down ladders like poisoned angels. For the past two years I've put everything that bites into this basket. The name of the snake book is *Sero*. Its elongated cylindrical body has no *apparent limbs.* The serpentine body is itself the appearance of a limb. The spotted, veined, marbled skin of my mother. The body is crisscrossed with hidden limbs, segments of sentences on the verge of a nervous breakdown.

I note the opiates mixed with honey, with syrup, with aloes. Soft pastes

A burst of laughter. Ten a.m. Or a bark? I listen. A laugh resounds, creeps, ricochets, coughs, floats up the stairwell, laughs, laughs, hiccups, makes a notch, falls back. Mummy! I murmur.

I write: Mummy! I will be able to write: Mummy! I will always be able to write Mummy.

Towards the end of the year I stopped sleeping over and over I repeated to myself a sentence my friend had said to me around July 15 of the previous year, I remember having made a note of it but I didn't remember where in which of my dozens of notebooks, some mornings I could spending hours hunting for it, which made my life sick, times and states mingling until my head was in a whirl, I couldn't find it, abruptly I put a halt to my frenzy, I said the sentence over to myself again as it seemed to me I had heard it, we were speaking of "courage" and of "two sides" I think I remember. Then the sentence had said: "Maybe I ought to convert." I said the sentence over to myself. Maybe it was "Perhaps I'll have to convert." But sometimes I thought I remembered he'd said "I think I must convert without delay." The variations were killing me. Over and over I repeated the word I had flinched at. As soon as he'd said the word *conversion* I'd been seized by a spasm of doubt. As if the hearing faculty had blacked out. The word *conversion*, I'm absolutely certain of it, this was the word upon which my presence of mind had failed me, instead of following the conversation, I went after the word conversion, which had instantly joined up with that other mighty word, the word "instructions." Names of things my friend had in mind all the time, and that I experienced like the words of a dream fading, gleaming from afar on the black waves, towards which one heads led by the conviction that they have the explanation, unstable glow-worms flickering, shifting, seductive to which we trust for it is probable they have the secret. I remember having felt the brief expiration of the enigma on my brow. An inflexion of urgency in my friend's voice. Perhaps I could have asked him what he meant, but this I believe was impossible. He didn't say this sentence to me I tell myself. He said it to himself just as on the phone you talk to yourself through the other. I went quiet. Maybe I was wrong. It seems to me he was in a rush. As if he said "Perhaps I should go right now and convert." "We'll discuss this again," he'd said. For me that meant both that he would speak to me about it, and wouldn't speak to me about it or that he believed he'd spoken to me about it and would speak to me, both, what it meant was: wait for me here I'll be back.

Right away I wondered what *conversion* meant. I could come up with a thousand interpretations. In every version of the word I could see the difference of this or that "conversion" from itself, no thinking word so convertible as the word conversion in every sense of the word each with its own divergence from itself, with its true its false which are neither true nor false, I could also imagine thousands of hypotheses within the difference itself. Naturally I didn't ask him when we would talk "about this" again. Naturally never afterwards did I ask him if he'd converted one way or the other. What was at stake was *a conversion.* Which one? I wondered. We'll discuss this again, he says. And the subject never came up again of course.

I may have thought it had slipped his mind. I may have thought the time would come. I may have thought I'd invented the phrase. I may have thought I'd dreamed it, this was plausible, it does happen that I no longer know whether certain events happened in reality or in a dream. What might have made me think that all this happened in a dream was the extraordinary intensity and the extraordinary uncertainty that emanated from the words, a supernatural synthesis of uncertainty intensity, a red-hot combination of the two. Over time the phrase acquired the intensity of The Word. Eventually, what with rubbing the natural possibility of questioning my friend about the sentence against the natural impossibility, I spend hours mulling it over.

"How could I not have asked him? How could I have renounced his answer, how could I have lost it?" I asked myself. And right away I pushed the question off to one side, as hard as I could, I saw it as a hydra, I tried to shut the door. I could have given myself hundreds of answers, none of which would have calmed the immensity of the regret that roared in my breast each time I told myself I should have asked him. Whereas each time he'd uttered this or that enigmatic phrase in my hearing, talking to himself through me, I naturally began by telling myself that above all I should not ask him what he meant. I know perfectly that he left one of those kaleidoscopic propositions there on purpose, I told myself. He himself might have a preference for this or that interpretation, maybe he has no preference whatsoever, he would let me choose or not, he leaves me to choose, he lets me choose or not choose or not, such is his vital flexibility. Whereupon I thought just the contrary. Perhaps he hid a key. And I don't see it. But at that point I might tell myself that he knew *or* didn't on the other hand know I didn't see. Since I said nothing. I wondered what he would have said, I mean what he would say, if I were to tell him what sort of internal labyrinth

I had embarked upon, and I knew exactly. He would have told me: just ask *me*. I knew it. Not to be able to ask the question which it is permitted to ask, this impotence I could not get into my head. It is and it cannot be. It makes me ill. I had a dream about it.

In a manner totally unexpected my friend had at last stopped by to say that having an appointment in Paris he couldn't stay but he'd be back. He couldn't tell me when exactly. When it's over he says. I begin to wait. A strange bliss whose other heart is pain. This time I tell myself. This time I'm going to ask him. It's all I can think of. Little by little time catches fire. Each hour goes by This means I tell myself that he is busy.

Unfortunately my conviction that he'll be back "when it's over" has slowly been eroded by an anguish of doubt seeping in under my skin

In the meantime I'm prey to gloomy thoughts *intus et in cute*. I'm consumed by the desire to talk to him. I need to tell him there is a crush of questions I didn't get to ask. Unfortunately among needs I am at odds with myself. I must not fail to ask him my questions this time but the idea of satisfying this need horrifies me. I argue with myself endlessly. When he finally does turn up, I'm tongue-tied with anxiety. He'll go away in the end I tell myself and everything will be over for eternity, including eternity. All the same, even miserable, I am wildly conscious of my good fortune. I wanted urgently to ask: was the fact that he's alive maybe proof of the famous *conversion*? Could and should I think I was face to face with a "conversion" success story? I wanted to ask him: should I think of you as a convert to dreams? Was this the sort of conversion his phrase had been hinting at? I trembled with terror at the thought that he was not converted, but just a dream. Were this the case, best that I, in my eagerness, not disturb the illusion. Finally I said that if I could, I should like to ask.

Immediately appalled at the thought of the consequences, I start to say to you that if it were possible maybe you might tell me where you had been, and what you'd been doing, though I wouldn't, above all, wish this to deprive you of the least bit of freedom, of lightness, I was wretched, was I not committing the irreparable blunder, would the best thing not have been since he was at that moment alive not to make any allusion at all to what at that moment was not, but in another way I feared offending him if I appeared to forget where he came from, and to act as if the unthinkable were not there yawning behind the door. Unfortunately I had no experience at all, no opinion. And I writhed in anguish at the very moment I found myself nonetheless in the world truer than truth with my friend. No, I tell myself, I must not yield to my absolute need to know. I don't know whether I want to know, I don't know whether I ought to know, I writhe with pain at the thought of not knowing, and I feel sure this anguish risks offending him and producing the fatal small shock to the dream. In the end I say: I am glad to see you. Me too, he says.

So long as he is alive, I tell myself, the dream is a blessing. We don't know what dreaming means.

What he doesn't know

– *There's a thing he doesn't know*, I say, I was shivering with cold, I had just *glimpsed the start of something invisible* that I was however able to see, starting off in the distance, in the upper reaches of the distances, I felt icy, as if I'd all of a sudden without warning crossed over into the cold century I had just had a clear glimpse of a global denaturing, as yet unnamed, contained in a section of indelible and cold blue sky, like a *replacing* of one world by another, a sort of cold version, withdrawn, inconceivable, that I could only call "thing," for this phenomenon was something I had just caught a glimpse of above me for the first time – and shattering, as shattering for instance as an *explosion* beyond the beyond the speed of sound, which would be terrifying because one would hear it only from the inside. Here's the new *Thing*, I told myself, and with a glance I pointed the Thing out to my daughter, in place of the sky, chilling it, that I felt in a flash. "That." The uniform blue canvas of the sky *mute* in the trees, I indicated with jerk of my chin, *that*, the still blue canvas of the silence that was snapping up the sky, but how to name that which does not exist and whose notexist one feels as the outcome of a supernatural Annulment like what the Thing might have been after God had erased the world with a swipe of his sponge: the unnameable of a never again in the aftermath of a never more

And *That*, I say, he doesn't know. If there's *one* thing he doesn't know, I say vaguely, it's this world – I was saying these words in a muffled voice – that one could take for a Cloud of silence.

– but the world, says my daughter in her to-the-rescue voice, the world, I remember in his final texts, he spoke of the world to come, says peace my daughter, he spoke to Europe with such insistence he called upon her, he wanted her to come, says my peace

– the world I say – I tried to name it, my thought banged its head against the mute blue thread stretched taut across the face of the sky all smeared with invisible, what is it called, what to call what he doesn't know I say the experience of the world with the telephone cut off, that's not what I meant, he would have detested, that is he would have stopped loving he would have de-attested hearing a new noise: the inaudible explosion of the silence that follows the cutting off of the world-telephone and that

he doesn't know the unbearable-to-the-senses thunder of the si lence of that which one no longer sees – my thoughts were wandering radar gone astray radar leading astray that which I was attempting to sketch, a world of effacement, the worldwide canvas of the withdrawal, nature without before without after, lopped off, the state of the-world-lopped-off – *l'émondé* – the beggared-world – *l'émondicité*

herecomes some Thing he doesn't know, the Thing he causes, a state of place he brought into the world in resigning it

the paralysis of time

the cattle car of the world packed with the war-wounded

a stillness of the air not a sound-wave nor a shadow of a wave nor streak of syllable nor silence of echo,

air that immobilizes

state of God who has spit himself out

but of course I could say the contrary and thereupon think the contrary and thereupon believe it, that he knows one way or another what he doesn't know, from an innate aptitude to know also what he doesn't know, from an ability to be able to do what he lacks the power to do, I can think that, I don't believe it, he can do anything but know the thing stopped the without striking, what am I saying, the without without, the cavernous immensity the immensimmobility of the flat, the flat world, the infinite immeasurable plain of the world emptied of time all tenses of all the verbs vanished

what were you saying about the world I say

– it was very striking that business around the theme of hope for Europe and alterglobalism says indefatigable my daughter

what were you saying that he said I say ten times

and ten times she responds indefatigable presence, over there there's some there-is-ness, I push the button and she responds

– the empty world is filled with emptiness I say, but this world left here, a flattened cosmic placenta is totally void of void, the real true world, Great World, is void of master void-void ravished of its principal inhabitant, its thinker its thinker-healer, the realtrueworld, Eye Void the Great is today the day on which I write in the year that follows, the in-vain year, the year neither straight ahead nor towards, the year of the spark put out, sharp and matt. Dries itself up.

Herein ends.

Fall of the words *here*, *come*, *if*, *who knows*,

but I could feel the contrary and when I can feel the contrary I will be able to say it

this being-ableness, this reason-ableness, that depends upon being's effort to resuscitate

physically situated in my pleura, which is where the will's breath takes shape,

The mornings especially are difficult. They dig in their heels. They keep themselves to themselves. The expression "one fine morning": quite the opposite. "One fine morning" is how the world begins again. And next something happens, if the morning is fine. Or just the opposite: if something happens, the morning is fine. Mornings vile, shrew-faced. I get up. The world's not there. Day does not dawn. I don't believe. Six a.m. Belief does not show up. Belief is downstairs, in the house, in my mother's room. It doesn't climb upstairs to me.

The anguish is the morning's. The house is empty. I live in the void.

My beloved is off on the other side of the world in Manhattan, it's not the same day.

I have no apparent limbs. Nothing proves my mother is sleeping downstairs.

Her not-a-sound is already here.

An endless despair which is itself endlessness inhabits all the rooms of my thought. Where are the children and the childhoods? I am cut off from life. It has gone abroad. Or I am abroad. Night has dropped me off abroad. On an island. I can't get back on foot not even barefoot. Where are my children and their childhoods? You cannot imagine how vast the distance between two floors is when the soul is deprived of speed. Yet every morning the cats get me up. That's their job. They walk on me pawing scratching till I resurrect. But the world has not yet turned up. This delay disembodies me. Voids me. The envelope is full of ghosts. Sad images of the future past of the future time past, time so far past it can't turn back. The two cats on their nests. They brood over life. Meanwhile I cling to the baskets of life. Too early to summon the living to my aid. I can't myself do that.

But the books speak.

I sit with books beside me, before me, behind me, up to my shoulders in them, dozens of them, hundreds perhaps, most of them lying down, arms wide they remember everything.

– Who?

The telephone. My son the mathematician and kindness. Kindness is mathematical.

– There is no world, I say. It makes me ill. – Has anything like this ever happened to you? – No. I'm not here, I say

– That I know, says the kind mathematician. Set theory begins with a primitive object.

– I don't know whether I'm a primitive object or if it's the world. I see the world I say and I can't jump on

– One sees something says my son but one sees nothing

– What do I do? I say – Slow down and try a little inertia says my son the exister.

I feel better having an illness that can be analyzed.

At 10:30 invisible my mother lets out a nice long laugh. Invisible long laugh. Encore. Laugh for me, I think, only for me. Again she laughs. I've been heard. From a distance. A long wild laugh.

I go down. The laughter draws me. Moves me. The thirsty go to the spring as to the temple. She is not where I think she is. The closed door of her room. I open. A crack. She is lying on her bed, pale, eyes closed, meager arms freckled. I think: one fine morning, that's when a Toofast crashes into the towers, and a second later boom another one. Her eyes open. Silence. Smile. What I do: furiously I leaf through the face, examine it, sample it, palpate. She sees me. She looks at me. She notices my avidity. She says:

"Are you looking for Titine?"

Who is Titine? My mother? Death? The proof? I ought to have asked her.

As long as my mother is here my friend is still living, I tell myself. I keep her here. I waste her. I don't sit with her to watch her watching television. The beans. The chard. The rice. Nothing's any good. Says she. I go back upstairs. I walk around on top of my mother. I try not to set my feet on her bed, on her body. I write.

She gnaws at her leash. She lifts her umbrella. She throws down her cane. You are cloistering me. You want to make me older than I am. Let me tell you something: you are forever reminding me we die in the end but what else is new? We are made to disappear. Obviously this is a thing we cannot conceive of. That's what life is all about. It's awful to be old. Always somebody reminding you there's no perspective. You see me with a beard of six long steel grey hairs on my chin.

I don't cling to her. I act as if I'm rich, spendthrift. I watch myself spend all the time. I don't slow down. I ascend to my paper nest. I gaze out over the head of the world. In the background, beyond the world the forest opens and emptiness begins

– I laughed because of that Lance Armstrong fellow, now he's taking Viagra, all the big guys take Viagra. She laughs till she cries, lying in bed, immense, she grows and grows, the world shrinks, all those insects who take Viagra. On the other hand what flabbergasts her is the monumental malice of crooks. All things considered as far as people go there are two kinds: insects so tuckered out they take Viagra, and the rest, all those people one doesn't know, snakes, *môlosses*, *wahtch dahgs*, you know what a *môlosse* is? She lounges on her bed above the world abyss and she sucks up the unspeakable horrors of Balzac's *Cousin Pons* with the delight of an immortal. Unbelievable what goes on! It bugs me. People like that and we never meet them. In any case I'm not in the business. She is pleased with herself. Quit scratching I say. She's popping the blisters. Those are *your* blisters I say. She scratches the arms very fast. Stop scratching the arms I say, they're yours. We do not know ourselves. Now she's getting his money! That Cibot woman. Nothing stops her. She who looks after them with such devotion. It's frightening. She laughs. How dreadful Creation is! Hard to believe such people exist! Unbelievable. She's lucky at her age that she's managed not to have anything to do with the Cibots of this world. The minute the midwife she hired for the Clinic brought her croissants that was the end *oh-ver*! Croissants? Out! She knew right away what was up. The two nutcrackers, a pair of dopes! Monsieur Pons! All his bile poor man is in this book. I can understand people don't want to read it. I can understand people do. Thirty pages left. Still, she would glad if he lived. Anyways, she says, he has to go on living to the end otherwise the book can't be called Monsieur Pons. Therefore she can go on reading since the book is called Monsieur Pons she will always be able to go on reading, I trust

What am I saying? All life is on my mother and my friend's side. She calls me, I respond, she doesn't hear. I shout: Yes! I'm here! I'm coming! I'm coming! They don't hear me. It's me, it's my voice my mother doesn't hear. I go up, I come down, I run as fast as I can, from the bottom of my being I shout: I'm coming! I'm coming! Oh! The crazed voice, driving me crazy. In the trees. Down below. On the phone. Finished the simulacrum! No longer do I pretend not to be riddled with fears. Where are you? I cry. I throw myself into staircases, into the outer rooms, needless to say I no longer know who is to be saved, her, him, safe, save, saved, him or her, it seems to be me, to be her, that it's you, one wants to save, to save, one doesn't know where, one runs as quick as one can as if one could get there in time where are you? she calls. At last I glimpse a wisp of your hair coming round the corner of the hall, I throw myself after you in German, I shout *Hier bin ich. Ich bin da.* That is to say. All this is incredible. What a state you are in!

Frightful. Here I am. I say: Here I am. I hear: Here I am. Never has this phrase been so pleading, so pitiful. What a state you are in! I say. And she seems to excuse herself, saying: But I'm here, here I am. I take you in my arms. In truth you are double. One might think that the other is me, that I myself am mixed up in this. What's more you cling to me. You have a fearful double, unrecognizable, face fixed, as if frozen, expressionless and you yourself are off to one side behind, I look after the two of you, I guess that this is what must be done in such cases. Oh! As if I didn't know what state you are in.

"*Titine,*" *says my mother* is when you work yourself into a state about something before or after it happens. Doddering old lady, I see you. Always looking for trouble. You think I'm old *differently*. But my joints are all in working order. She is still lying on the bed. She nibbles chocolates. Titine says my mother that means: you've come to check on the patient?

I treat myself to a chocolate

And what do I see: you're the one who's sick. You're not about to get over your fear

You lock yourself in and turn the key twice

You bury your cat

You weep twofold and for tomorrow

– But what makes you burst out laughing? I say

– The voice of wisdom: we never listen to it, I'm thinking about Monsieur Pons she chuckles. You you're always in advance. The others always late. With you around no one's in danger of not wasting their time waiting for what will only happen only at the end. And Balzac– there's another one, says my mother. The way he understood the vileness of people, me people who aren't on the up and up right away without a second thought I show them out but Balzac waits. That Cibot, the concierge, with her croissants and chocolates, I show her out.

Still, he did find a couple of innocents the German and that Monsieur Pons fellow and the rest of them are krooks. That poor man all the foul tricks those people played, he had them in his head, she bursts out laughing, he must have had tons of people on his back, all those krooks *on his back* reading him, and the tricks *in his head*, she laughs, and all the same he found two innocents, it reminds me of the krooks your father the innocent always had around him and you too, surrounded, Bernhard likewise is not a happy man that restaurant full of eatallyoucan countyourpennies folks who were down on their luck and didn't watch their step, they get sucked dry, later they take to books. The locked doors at your place don't surprise me in the least. She laughs I'm thinking about this poor Monsieur Pons, it's a bit much, innocent okay but not to that point. All that woman's floozy flattery in my house I'd have put a halt to it. A few chocolates is all it takes, chocolates no thanks, out! Strange your father was so trusting. He's *incapable* of believing in the vileness of others, he knows but he can't believe. I still haven't got over that. And the upshot is everyone's dead. And *all the goods* shared among krooks. When I think of it, that poor Schmuck who slept in a maid's room. Makes me laugh. Poor guy he wasn't up to it. No match for his assailants. She lies down flat on her back, in which position the laughter spurts out stronger, she pops two chocolates. I'm laughing because this hasn't happened to me. Lucky for Monsieur Pons they made him a fine coffin. If he'd only known, poor man! He came to his senses *just a little too late.* Balzac though, even at the notary's he knows what's what. The notary took you to the cleaner's too you and your children. When one goes to see the notary one can expect the worst she laughs to tears he even did in our poor clerk he even totally *did him in*, the clerk *vanished* and the new one got you into a fine mess three idiots the sale of that studio you were had three innocents I mean idiots. That three people could be had! One, I can understand. You have no idea what I'm talking about.

Had, that's what you are! You are writing? But I know what I'm talking about

Now that I've done with Monsieur Pons she chuckles she pushes away the plate of chocolates, I need to read Colonel Whozit.

– Another idiot I say. – Poor fellow says my mother. Unfortunately that's your sweet literature for you. A ship of fools who come to their senses *a little too late.*

I look at her she has grown larger again differently. I say: "You are looking very pretty" but it's not that. It's. The charm of an involuntary and fluvial grandeur, some principle that blazes in her eyes, as if her whole being were at the windows. You look pretty I want to defend my point of view to her eyes, but I don't know what to call the light I mean the victory I mean the sound of laughter I mean – the frame says my mother, the hair's still good – yes yes the hair I'm fond of my thick, strong, stubborn hair, but it's not that. It's the way you are in danger of crossing over to the other side at the wink of an eyelash. But I don't say it. The wide long lashless lids flutter.

You are pretty, I say and she believes me.

– I'm getting on but I haven't aged. What I don't understand is this dizziness which is not dizziness. A lack of balance. Lucky for me the shopping cart still gets me around better than the umbrella. Whereas you. Yet another incalculable phrase, I tell myself. I note whereas you, the shopping cart, the umbrella, my mother

I come down with one illness after another

I come down with my mother's skin

I come down with the earth which goes away

I come down with the being of my friend who is everywhere

I come down with my brother's maladies

I come down with one cat then the other

I expect to come down with my daughter and of course it happens

I am ill with thought, I am on thought anti-inflammatory drugs, I do not for a second believe in the magic power of thought but it's not up to me

Let crazy terror take my head, nobody could fend off an attack more powerful than the idea of power.

It's not what one thinks it is. It's not what one doesn't think it isn't. It's not what one thinks it isn't. What is most unlikely is what's most probable. The unthinkable trembles my heart, I call it "fear! fear!"

The illness comes into being again, I change it, and all this without the slightest calculation. One day one the next the other. I'm convinced *I make* myself sick one illness after another without being able to do a thing about it. Thinking I know this is an illusion of the ill. It's no help at all my knowing it. All the same, no complacency. Each illness makes me doubly ill 1) with the illness 2) with being sick of being ill. Every time *I make* myself sick, I always make myself sick again but I see perfectly that I do this on the same model, it's always the end of being, generally it's at the bottom of the garden this happens, the way the death of my father took place, starting in the garden's northeast corner which suddenly fills up with this terrifying substance, invisible but substantial, tactile, perceptible perceived as brushing as growling, this colossal quantity of void that one hears sighing if one could hear it (but one doesn't want to, one is petrified), not breathing but sighing, as if the garden our daily body were suddenly occupied by a body too big diffuse internal and thus hollowing out of our usual compact and limited body bottomless pits of visceral caverns and this content, this monster is a nightmare in broad daylight without a hope of waking, the vanguard of Regret that already fills up all the available space, that spreads out into our eyes our throat our lungs great doses of bitterness and sobs to come. I am perfectly aware that the misfortune is my fault, I call upon no one, but taking advantage of my deficit of vigilance during sleep the illness spreads into every inch of me like a building going up without any estimation of its internal or external resistance and I am its even before I open my eyes. The minute I'm up, I lack everything, daylight, courage, sturdy legs, everything necessary to life: movement, confidence, habit, the solidity of things, the loyalty of vital beings! So far as I can see everything betrays me. No one I can count on. Death is the first to come along. I see it everywhere, far more overwhelming than my mental debility and it picks and chooses, according to probability or improbability.

Nobody can fend off a hurricane, it grinds up and kills at random, that I am at the origin of it doesn't in the least lessen its impact. I *need* to yield. It needs to bite. It requires its all but daily carnage.

Almost every day I can feel myself suffering mainly in the head, I can explain the pain to myself but knowing it comes from an inflammation of my imagination doesn't prevent it being reality itself. What's more I'd be crazy not to go crazy. We don't know what an illness is. On awful hurts we plaster little old words, as if we could think hell with a paper bandage.

Every time I come down with another disease, I suffer from horrible aches and pains in my head, the container, contents and idea, I suffer from the power that my head and especially my thought processes have over my head, over my body, I very quickly find myself suffering globally, the narrow seam of the skull box and the imaginations box communicate, I regret losing my head to a disease this is a defeat for me and for others. Which doesn't mean I give in. On the contrary, I'm off and running. Watch me: throw myself on the phones, on the roads, call my brother the doctor, even in another country I call him, call my father the doctor, even in a country other I call him, call my vets and my dead, everything one can call and everything one can run after everywhere.

– Yesterday you mourned for a cat that was perfectly fine, says my mother. Off you run to the witchdoctor. State of mourning decreed for the day. You inter your cat in the pink of health. What a temperament! Always running down under the earth. Never with your mother. And you do it again. And again.

When I'm twisted with pain, I do hear my mother's words, and marvel at the spirit that speaks from her invisible professorial chair. Even the idioms come down from on high, she may quote philosophers she's never read, or maybe it's that she's read them in the dregs of my heart.

Today it's not wrong to say that yesterday I buried my cat before it was too late, I say. But yesterday this wasn't yet so. Yesterday I did see death coming, and I wasn't the only one. The cat saw, and I saw what Philia saw for we communicate bodies and fears. I examine what's wrong. Down in the dumps, limp, flattened, her therefore me. Shut in, abandoned, flat on the bed in the grips of the malady. Not that, I say. I can't I say. Don't take her from me I say. I look at the path on which she is not frolicking. I'm not making this up I say. Death is after me again. Me, I wait two weeks says my mother. The cat planted in my heart, the enemy lodged right next door. Nothingness slowly rises up in the garden. I've already been through this and succumbed. I realize. I reread "Psychoanalysis Searches the States of Its Soul." It's beginning again says my friend. And on this we agree. For instance, says he, cruelty. You've always got time says my mother. Time has us I say. I grab the cat and I start to run like a madwoman. Flags half-mast, says my mother. She laughs. I can't stay seated faced with immobility. The first thing I can't do is write: I can't stay seated. I have to run. I run to the witchdoctor. I race to the vet. At the same time

I am running so as not to remain seated in the midst of the cruelty. I run to *keep* Philia from sitting speechless without moving in front of the door. The deepest pit of horror is to *see* dying. One can't conceive of greater pain: see life ebb and be unable to hold onto it. One is nailed down. One pleads. I un-nailed myself. I swept up the cat. With all my strength I raced down the path where she was already not frolicking. I ran for ages. Meanwhile you act as if you believe in witchcraft. In the beginning I ran for two for the cat hence for me, I was running at once for the living and for the dead. Saying that I was burying my cat isn't wrong but in point of fact I was exhuming her.

All of a sudden she wakes up, she takes a sip of breath, purrs, slinks off.

Am I resuscitated? Not yet. I take great strides along the edge of the world, the figures of death lurk at the grills, still a little nothingness in the garden, behind the curtain.

I don't write.

We are all thinking of death in this house we are all thinking of the death that is already ensconced in the house but we are so busy fighting it, punching it in the arm in the stairwell, my brother puts his whole weight on its back and pins it down crushes it but how much longer can we hold it off

We all think of death she is at the door she rings the bell

Ten o'clock. A downpour. In the rain the downstairs shutters bang. She's alive. Until 10 o'clock I struggled. I wanted to go down. Mental silhouettes barred the stairs, the ghosts of everything and everything's opposite.

Anguish after happiness, anguish: aftermath of happiness.

Yesterday I still had my three little ones, my children, my cats, my babies, my friends, all those one calls "little ones, tiny little ones" to shield them from the eye of the disaster. And now it's pouring, if the shroud of the world is made of rain, this is the storm that invented it. All that is reposes under a mournful-colored sheet. I can no longer find my little ones. The thunder gives no one the right to utter a cry even my mother in her armchair doesn't let out a peep. Could it be the visit of the former owner that sends them off in all directions? On the walls of the kitchen hearts are stopped. The farmer, the man who used to own the land, has come he says to hand over the deed of sale. What makes an owner go out where no one who holds life dear would venture is beyond me. Which is why, because of the two attacks from without, I am on my guard. He explains to me, the farmer, that he *liquidated the cemetery* that was in a field. – And the dead? Did you take them away? I worry about the dead. The idea they've been evicted. And in this end-of-the-world weather. It makes me sick. The farmer says *he has seen to it*. Yet another heartache. Meanwhile, having slipped into the timeless kitchen, my own, my little ones disappear, they stray off into the big world, straws blown hither thither without a trace. Off I go after them, I call to them. Calling is my destiny. I shout the names up streets down fields, I search on all fours in forests I look under cars, in mud puddles, pretty soon I turn into a diluvian piece of human bread good for meatballs for the dead. Furthermore I don't give a damn I am the one who has lost her children and I am looking everywhere for them with Despair as a stick to drag through the mud. No one helps me, no. What I turn up in the heap of rags and debris that clogs the boulevard is not a little one, it's my hat, proof that I've already been here and for nothing

later, some other evening, I shall find among the streets and tables head down feet in the filthy air five minutes before it gets meat-hooked on the block, my plumpest little one, a clever child fattened on dreams of a future who as a baby in the midst of disaster was already able to talk about what he hoped to do when he grew up. Opera singer. I pounce on him, here's one I shout, the shout snaps in my throat, one of three, more pain, red-colored pain, that fellow won't be safe and sound so long as the rest are still missing, I hug him to the point of encrustation, one of three is nevertheless one divided by three, I search, I search, rain rain in the black rain two dark little bodies my pretty ones perhaps but no two goggle-eyed little owls so it goes I lose my children I mean my cats I mean my eyes I mean Mummy I mean me I mean

The last word

– You're digging caves under my bed says my mother, when she gets mad she's as tough as ever and the truth is on her side. I could say the opposite. She's the one who's digging under my bed. I sleep on death row. I am furrowed by the death in which she is going to let go of me. I cannot live without: *forgetting*. This means mustering up a strength of will one doesn't have and at the very moment one doesn't have it one takes a giant step out of one's head and one has it. I spend half my life feeling grateful to her, this gives me an excuse to kiss her hands, I mean the skin on her hands, the arms dappled with leopard spots, plunk kisses on her cheek, which is like finding somewhere on the slender remaining vertical surface to set your lips, her temples, her lips, I can never get enough kisses, it's an insatiableness, gladly she allows this, I see I make haste lest she melt.

I cannot tell my mother that more and more when I'm expecting Mummy my grandmother turns up, the fiction is not a fiction, my mother is turning into my grandmother; her youthful side turns up only on rare and distant occasions. Last night, for instance, when I miraculously managed to push the bathroom door open with my shoulder and catch my mother going on fifty. Oh! how I recognized her, behind her back I shuddered. This is Mummy in the prime of life, already I saw again the blunt strength of her arms, of her neck, which I hadn't seen for so long that seeing them again I could measure the bottomless pit of forgetting. Had I not banged into that door, the young, sturdy, foursquare woman who appeared to me, would have been gone forever, vanquished, eliminated by my present mother-character. She pleased me. But the sores! She has enormous sores on her body that she is carefully cleaning, absorbed in her meticulous work with the air of a dog utterly given to licking itself. So she didn't hear me crack open the door and take a step onto the threshold of the secret. It's the first time I've taken my mother's life by surprise. Thus she will have kept quiet and behaved her whole life as if she must owe nothing to anyone. Soon it will be fifty years that she has been keeping mum. The pride and vigor of this attractive woman, much bigger and stronger than my mother who preceded her, of whom she is the illegible remains, I saw for the first time and I might never have seen them. I was elsewhere, then. I don't even know when this remarkable being gave up wanting to be noticed. I didn't know at what point in time she severed herself from her height, from her promise, in order to go stooping under time's porch and, uncrowned, dethroned, find herself on the other side, divested of her former powers and without anyone to speak for her lost splendor, not even me, not even herself and no Villon. And then I pushed the door closed without saying a word and I kept the image that had turned destiny inside out for me, like a letter returned to sender after the end. But this happens only once. The scene glimmered with the burning sad light by which one recognizes moments that wear their own mourning. I knew that I wouldn't see it again. I didn't struggle. I felt ashamed.

Now the person that I'm used to call Mummy in my dreams is the one who was my old grandmother when Mother was fifty or so. I call: Mummy! in she totters on her little feet, one size smaller than average, and the minute I see her enter I realize that I am looking at the appearance of my grandmother to whom my mother has little by little yielded, my mother lets my grandmother go by not that my grandmother is or has ever been the stronger of the two, on the contrary, what's catching up with my mother is a frailty she never had, which was my grandmother's in the days when she was on the way out, without the least opposition from me, slowly obeying the distant very distant very powerful (and too low-pitched) whistle of death, a song so grave, so low-pitched that it is inaudible to all but to the old and those whose deafness is attuned to the guttural call of a whale. In reality I always think I see my mother but whenever I half-close my eyes I see my grandmother trotting along where I expect my mother, as if my grandmother had escaped me on one side, my mother on the other, and I can't keep myself from welcoming and rejecting this bringer of bad news who moves me and whom I love. I reproach myself with being the victim of an hallucination to which I succumb.

My grandmother was so small we had the kitchen and bathroom built to fit her tiny person, and ever since then we have been bending down and ruining our backs to shrink to the size of my grandmother who is of a rare diminutiveness. In the end while she goes off, diminishing, she becomes a miniature big person, closing in on a hundred she at last reaches the height of a six-year-old child. This does not fail to enlarge the supremacy of her authority. Power belongs to the smallest and to the dead.

I don't dare tell my mother that I see my grandmother when I think I see her. I don't dare tell my mother that when I call her, my grandmother returns from the dead with their unsteady steps. My grandmother has been effaced. She wasn't during her reign. Mummy talks and talks, all the time. She goes back a hundred years. From ten in the morning until evening she acts all the parts, hundreds of people enter and exit the dining room, occasionally so as to go faster she recalls five together with the same name. Occasionally I jump off the tale still moving and return to my ghosts. Occasionally she doesn't talk at all. She has left. She's off on one of her trips. We'll come across her on a black dromedary or in a

Patagonian ocean playing midwife to whales. The baby is as big as the table, she says. As the dining room I say. We find her at Waterloo. She is collecting the wounded. She has her midwife bag. For everyone.

My grandmother of old is happy, contemplating the sunset. She says: *Ich hab'Sonne im Herzen.* She is alone with the sun.

Both of them suck on chocolates. I feel guilty. I suck my fault, it is bitter. Seeing my mother dissolve into my grandmother is doubly blasphemous, a cruel simplification, an attack on what in the world is dearest to me. I am sick of death and worst of all this sickness feeds on itself, the more afraid I am the more I am afraid the more I flee the more I am afraid the more I am haunted. I wake with a start trembling I run to check on my mother and I accuse myself of trembling and checking. She's hard to wake. She lies on her right side. I say Mummy! Mummy! Who knows how far she's gone. Her hair has grown. I lift a heavy colorless fringe. I kiss her forehead. I see myself lift up a lock of her hair. I see myself kissing her wan forehead. Finally she opens her eyes. But not her lips. God knows where she's been. Her eyes are saucers. Later I'll see these huge brown glimmering submissive eyes. Finally she opens her lips. The colorless lips. She says: Pretty maid, pretty maid, where have you been? Since she hasn't any teeth the syllables melt in her mouth. She smiles. She says: I'm getting up.

I look at her and I am seen. Her eyes follow me. She detects the state of my soul. She translates. I can't escape her. She is my judge and plaintiff. If I could look at her I could translate her. But all I can do is see her and flee myself. Once outside I close the door.

Once the door is closed I'll still see how, while the body faded and effaced itself, all the life washed up into the eyes that had never been so vast, so luminous, final last reservoir of the inalterable essence we call youth, and which goes on with its work of the starry gaze when the skin is nothing but a washed-out sack.

I'm in the wrong religion. I hinder my mother. I engineer, I make deals, I abhor this inflamed rusefulness, this compulsive contagious spying. I can't complain about the nail in my head. I invent it, I've invented it, I pound it into my temple, then I take anti-inflammatories. The foot. I trap my foot as well, for a change one day the temple the next the foot, I crush my toe. Thus I descend trembling, limping to check on my mother in the middle of the night. Limp, limp, *boite*, *boite*, I jingled, I hear everything, nothing changes, I spy the boxes nesting in all the boxes, *les emboitements*, even my car when I want to get out of the city even if it's to go and visit my love my life, scarcely have I slammed the door, it's too elegant a black metal box, much too flat and well-upholstered. Trap, trap, *âmeçon*, soul-hook, it would be better to give up sleeping, give up waking give up running, not budge, not think not remember not try to forget any more no more rotting no more fearing no more cherishing what lures the bad thoughts

And yesterday July 29 I decided I'd done with the *nothingnesssurvival synthesis*. I decided I'd done with the vise fear of losing losing out of fear. I'm going to cut the dizzy feeling in half down the middle. I can no longer see my mother totter along the path without falling over. I made up my mind the only possible way out was to break and convert, because *there's no other way out*. Lately every time I rush out of a university building, a theater, a neighborhood, every time I head for the emergency exit, all of a sudden I'm on the other side and not a soul in sight. No one in sight and I am alone, everybody else went out the same side all but me. I thought I'd gone out the right side, like everyone else. I led the way, I was ahead, I didn't follow anyone, I thought they were following me. The minute I went out, it all happened. I found myself on the other side of the building in the space-without-being, where it's clear nothing slips through, nothing happens, no point hanging around. Your mistake is telling yourself that if you cut across the space-without-being to save time, and take a right at the first corner, you'll end up back on the side of the others. I make it. I know it. The law of mistakes is that you go ahead and make them. I am heading straight for Error I say to myself and off I went as if gusts that I knew drove me away from my salvation swept me through the empty streets.

Suddenly I'd had *Enough* and this was no turn of phrase but a warm body, nervous, with a constitution I could count on like a younger brother. That's when I told my mother: on the other side it's really rather underdeveloped. We're going back. Really, I said: I want to go back, not possible unless Mummy who is part of me comes too. We wait in the empty street at the stop for Lethe, the only bus that runs both ways. My mother is losing patience. The bus doesn't come. It's not easy to wait for a bus you've heard is the only one that runs both ways. I check the guidebook. Neither Canto XIV of the *Iliad* nor Canto XI of the *Odyssey* mentions this place. Just what you'd expect for Lethe I tell myself. Naturally Forgetfulness attracts attention to itself by means of absence and omission. But for my mother the bus not turning up is the theme of her nightmares. I explain that in this country one comes along every quarter hour it's the best you can do, which she doesn't understand. We have to stay right here at the bus stop I say. Where's the quartered hour? she wants to know. I point to our stop. It's a sort of railed-off area, two meters wide, long spikes protruding from the middle of nowhere. In this flat space without any volume, desert deserted even by the desert, only the stop with all its spikes sticking up breaks with the absolutely nothing. To signal to the vehicle that one wishes to board Oblivion Return one must fan open the grille by pushing a button and lighting up the small lantern on the top of the archway, which I did. It's the one gleam of hope in this world. Still the bus doesn't come. That's when – just at that dire moment when I feel I'm about to lose control over Mummy – a young woman, nice, polite, trustworthy-looking, joins us at the stop, which gives me self-confidence. Proof I'm not wrong. Unfortunately help came too late. Mummy was on the verge of losing her temper. She wasn't listening to me any more. Suddenly wrenching herself from my side she flings at me that she's going to find a taxi, in this land with absolutely no means of transport. She crosses what is not a street but an accentuation of our disagreement that she calls street. I want to stop her. Since even the strongest of wills are weak on this side, she raises shadows of arms and cries shadows of words. I had to restrain her. But I couldn't leave the stop for fear the bus might come along. I called out to her. I called the way one calls only in dreams of desolation, howling at the empty sky a name one knows lies hidden beyond the reach of the human voice, a long dragged-out high-pitched cry even at the risk of tearing one's throat, as if one wished to kill some thing that does not answer behind the curtain of sky. Off she goes. I called, my mother went off. With shaky steps she plunged into a stairwell, a black mouth of which I saw only the lip. I was afraid she'd fall. That's when I saw the Bus come along on it came steadily, ponderous as fatality. Make it wait! I begged the young woman. I wanted to think she'd hang onto Lethe I don't know how by the gills, by the hair, by the need to run as I myself would do, as I myself did. I dashed after Mummy. One stops thinking. Standing above the staircase chute halfway down I made out a collapsed little body, shapeless, rolled up into a fold of time. A gentleman, sober-looking, elegant, like all those who must pronounce the unbelievable, tells me: "Your father has *fallen*."

'*Your father has fallen.*" That's all I need, that's the last word, the key, I tell myself. I murmured the phrase over and over. I wondered what my friend would have thought of it, of the Your father, of the word it ended on, "fallen," of this very proper gentleman, this obsequious personage who had it would appear been posted here to pronounce these words to me, or to announce the news in the shape of a sentence, and who was himself a perfect match for the phraseology. I wondered what my friend would have said of this *fin mot*, this last word, this end word, of its finesse, its finesses, its finality, its lastness. Meanwhile I racked my brain for what had been my mother's last word crazed with anguish I searched, what was the word and when did she say it, I had the ghastly feeling I was the one who'd done all the talking lately, I don't count Mummy's pointed remarks, which were in any case copies of my own unspoken ones, and then and there, on the threshold, I began to fear I had again missed the crowning word, dolor without end, irremediable. Then I wondered what my friend would have to say about a title like "Your father has fallen" for this book in which it was again and again endlessly a question of suffering living, of the suffering of living, after hearing a sentence as appalling and incomprehensible as that which the gentleman had addressed to me, articulating each syllable, what would he say, I asked myself, for it struck me that this notification was like the summed-up wormwood core of all I'd been subjected to lately, and it seems to me he would say "That's a dream of a title," which was absolutely true. I wondered what he would think of this book, which was a bane and a pale on which I skewered my heart, and whose cruelty, to which he'd attached his name his work his life, of late, was one cause.

All these thoughts swarmed around the sentence that I put off receiving, that I left hanging like a sealed envelope, that unhinged me. For I believed it even though I didn't understand it. I saw the little body stretched out on the formless step, plunged into the fold of some dim fabric, nothing to prove it was my mother. I was convinced of it.

It's Mummy. This silhouette like the last word of her transformations. I let the mother of my life, therefore my life, escape me, I told myself.

They tell me: "Your father has fallen" so as not to tell me the truth. Or, on the other hand: to tell me the truth. My mother who falls is my father. If my father was my mother, if my mother is my collapsed father, then I am the little brother of my brother, the feeble brother of the strong brother. My friend's presence is at my side. This is the end of life over here, or it's the crux, I remain standing, staggered, on the edge of the abyss. I don't go down the stairs: they've already changed my mother. The substitution is starting. Behind me Lethe steps on the gas and disappears. I don't jump aboard Forgetting. There's not a thing *to do.* That's what to remain is. Remain standing. Not touch the nothingness. My friend's presence stands at my side. I am on his right. He doesn't speak. Nobody moves. We are in amber. We are all here, somehow. A we is here.

I can't tell my mother that every time she runs away from me she drops me she is my fallen father

"Your father has fallen," this is the phraseology of war, you can fall without being fallen my friend would have said, yet another homonymy, dozens of times we spoke about this falling word, this *tombe*, generally in its catachrestic forms, when one falls metaphorically, this means a moral or religious failing he told me, men fall, women are fallen, the man is the lady-killer, the *tombeur*. But it was the first time anybody had used the phrase to me. War was declared.

Yesterday I was and I had. Five minutes ago. Yesterday revs its engine behind me and disappears. At the moment I am borne along by my mother who falls and my friend who is gone. I can't telephone.

The list of those I have yet to lose grows longer under my eyes.

All those who are and are more than me for me and are even more me than I myself, remain. Turn up. Happen to me. Are going to go away. They go, come, go. It makes quite a commotion at that intersection of the future and the past, which passes for the "present."

The list of those I have yet to lose grows longer under my eyes, unrolls its luminous cortege right to the back of the garden and disappears. Lately I see a golden haze around beings, the kind that usually only haloes the silhouettes of those who have gone. As if my eyes were filled with loss and I was the one who misted those around me and to whom I nod in advance the way one smiles at the denizens of photographs who smile back at us with the potent, sustained gentleness of my cats. But it's not an as if, no, it's a more truthful vision of what we are, beings promised and withdrawn, taken away and restituted but differently, but changed by this incessant to-and-fro-ing through time. Something impalpable, but perceptible to the eye, some particle of disappearance stays stuck to those who for us are everything, a diaphanous film that I could no longer avoid noticing and which produced a sort of spiritual attachment. I could argue with myself till I was blue in the face, trying to imitate the old day-to-day-life, I was less and less able to detach myself from those who people my list, starting with my mother. A day-to-day-life I remember I once had it, but like an abstract memory attached to that extraordinary idiomatic phrase. These days I am in a super-acute, a hyped-up life. It never goes to sleep.

And yet all the events of this hyped-up life seem to be cut from the hyperdream. All of them turn up accompanied by a voice that murmurs to my heart "it's not going to last."

My mother walks past me she is two meters away in pajamas she shuffles her feet on the floorboards on her head a blue plastic cap her eyes fixed on the door which is her sole object, she goes by, without seeing me. My mother goes by. "Mummy!" I say in a loud voice. She goes by dragging her feet without stopping in front of me, eyes on the door.

I cry out: Mummy! I hold out my arms – as if she could hear my arms. She keeps on towards the door with the slow regular shuffling step of a sleepwalker. She is not asleep. She doesn't hear me. The door. My mother has gone by. The beyond is now in the house. This is a hyperdream. Nothing more violently real. I see it, it's my mother of the past who goes by me in reality

The house now looks right out on the beyond. At any moment there may be a knock.

The "*conversion*" I tell myself. My friend's word comes back to me. I wasn't familiar with the other-life that is taking over my house, so recently but already taking up space and power in every direction and for whom I am a stranger. I have everything to learn. An inaccessible life with which I wasn't familiar, about which neither document nor received wisdom exists, which I'm beginning to have a feel for, without guide, for guide and master there are none, there never are, each instance of hyperdream life is utterly singular.

All the words I use to designate unknown states and circumstances in this otherlife are words of replacement,

– The beyond gives onto the house. One goes from one to the other by conversion. When I use the word conversion I know what I mean. It's a pass-key.

III

A LEAVE

When *all is lost* I say to my brother, then and only then, when you are on your last legs, *fichu*, that's when salvation may turn up, I say to my brother, for this I say two things are required: 1) that I know in my soul and conscience that not only *have* I nothing left to hope for, but that I no longer hope; 2) that there be some sort of salvation on earth or hereabouts, which is unlikely and naturally uncertain. It was a summer Saturday whose splendor was so insistent, so manifest it prompted me to bare my heart to my brother, who sat beside me, feet propped on the brow of the oak, a sort of secret in the trembling and uncertain freshness of its meteoric upsurge. An as-yet-to-be-identified object. An *event* which I had just begun to think – without daring to predict or plot – if it didn't vanish might perhaps prove as potent, as grave, as consequential, as revolutionary, as the meteoric event of the discovery of literature as reality in the courtyard of the Hôtel de Guermantes or of literature's reality, an event of such fantastic import that, staggering from the shock of a heel against an outcrop of cobblestone, all literature was forever changed, an event comparable to that, also linked to a slab of stone, of the reading of the tablets of the Law, at a time when for Sinai's narrator all was lost. True, my own event, which had taken place that very day, being in its very first hours though it seemed to me destined to grow beyond all measure and acquire at the end of some indefinite period of time the rank and potency of a miracle – unless it faded like a ghost at first cock-crow – seemed to me for the moment as fabulous as first setting eyes on a new continent, or the key at least to such a continent, at least for now. For, unable to believe and all the while believing, for the time being I restricted myself to a feeling of utter joy, I disallowed myself neither that nor disbelief. From age-old habit as well as that complicated calculation which leads us to share our elation with our brother, less to shower him with gifts than to ensure that his complicity give our own insufficient powers of elation a boost, and so that the other may shore up and consolidate our leap into the void of our bedazzlement, and while vaguely reproaching myself with *taking* my brother as witness to yet another of my extravagant expeditions, I couldn't stop myself. Truth to tell I told him nothing, I consulted him, not a matter for calculation. I got carried away. Doubtless I could count on his credulity, on my own credit record, on our similarities of temperament. I could never have counted on my mother, two words and my continent was sunk. I still had the taste of the event on my tongue. If this is not an illusion, I was thinking, then at long last it is the answer to death, it is the road to bliss *in* suffering, I've found it. If I've found it – what I saw as a series of acts of grace and gifts, was nebulous, astronomical, I saw nothing clearly and I have time, I tell myself.

Here are the facts: I have just seen my friend J.D. again.

– He had a leave, I tell my brother. I should have stuck to that. But I got carried away. I took a chance. – Do you think there might be leaves? I say. – There are weekend leaves for patients with chronic illnesses. It's legal within a structure. "Outside the structure?" I say. That's beyond my allopathic competence, says my brother. I was about to go on. I stopped.

It's as if my brother granted me a leave for the beyond of allopathy. We gazed into the enigmatic, bottomless blue, a hospital with no law and no chief medical officer. – Doyouremember Papa's Panama hat? I say. – I remember one day I took a tram to school. An elegant young man in a boater looked vaguely like Papa I stared at him yearningly, perhaps it's Papa I said to myself it was a Perhaps that set up a hum of electricity in the exact spot of my brain, I might have turned this semblance into Papa's presence, says my brother.

A *special leave:* that it be *special*, that my friend be let out of hospital for a *special leave* we are not for a second allowed to forget. Shocked by such an *unbelievable* event, as if a bolt from the blue had flipped the hourglass to believable, I flung on my clothes, still in shock, not a second to lose, and I ran to the designated address, along with my daughter, and S., C., F. and M., a few friends who just happened to be nearby. What was wonderful and painful in those hours, nearly a day, is that they were part of day-to-day-life, while the special leave was granted by the beyond, with the result that two vital worlds mingled in a bewildering synthesis of the ordinary with the extraordinary. Nothing solemn. Each of us however was aware of the cruelly precious value of each moment, each of us in our own way did all we could to ensure that each drop of blood, each breath, each word be distilled to the essential.

One detail: the hat (ridiculous initially; later it made sense). I had an off-white straw boater on the table beside the telephone when my friend announced the news. A high white hat and "who knows why" "as they say in Algeria" as my friend would put it later, I found myself holding it as I raced down the street, throwing on clothes as I went. I hand it to my daughter, while I do up my shirt. Once I'm done up, I take it back. It wasn't my hat, otherwise I'd have put it on. The stupid thing is that towards evening – after moments so simple and so beautiful I told myself if "that" can happen like that, "death" as they call it, about which we know absolutely nothing, if, I told myself, one has a right to "*special leaves*," everything would be different, I'll think about this later I told myself – meanwhile, discussing a million topics of the utmost importance, striding along, seeing him fatigued and resplendent, I let him carry my hat which he held by the brim, in his left hand, perhaps to relieve me of it. Afterwards, I found this hat silly, but at the time of the leave it felt perfectly in synch with the double life of this instant, as were chairs, tables, café terraces, notebooks (two, one light grey, the other with a red cover), grey suit, cell phones, once, however, the leave was over the image of this stupid hat, which wasn't mine, and which suddenly I was holding in my hand, then my friend had it in his, a hat of a kind they don't make any more, and that we – who knows why – were supposed to take turns holding, as if it had been entrusted to us by who knows who, caused me an embarrassment I hadn't had time to feel during the breathless time of the leave when all my strengths of minds could not suffice to live in the present moment and simultaneously retain the extraordinary succession of written and spoken messages, explanations, recommendations, this or that detail sometimes sketched out on the pages of the notebook, tales that tumbled out all the more feverishly as we were aware that every moment of the leave was counted. Otherwise, if a leave could last for more than one day, which is impossible, I could perhaps have made something of this hat in consultation with my friend. But the hat was the least of my worries. In the meantime, however, we kept hold of it, no one could say it weighed more than a piece of paper. My sense of prudence dictated that I hold onto the hat and that I find myself in the end with this piece of headgear perched on the vestiges engraved to perfection in me, and down to the very last comma,

of the famous dream entitled *A Leave*. A dream which was in itself a leave good for one day on both sides.

So there may be leaves! Twenty times I said this to myself. Dreams – I've had a ton of dreams since the phone was cut off, I could write a book. But this time it was a *special* leave: *nothing like a dream*. We were aware of reality, of its laws, of history, of time, of duration, and we'd agreed, without quibble, since it was he who warned me he was on leave, this finite infinity that left to my own devices I'd never have allowed myself to hope for since he'd be the one to do all the work: the travel, customs and immigration, security checks over here, but above all, horrid moment I put off thinking about, which we never discussed, it would have been madness, his return to a beyond that he named, euphemistically, and alluding to his world famous writings on hospitality: the hospital. In a flash we understood how it worked, the structure. *Everything* we did and exchanged in our old day-to-day-life we did and exchanged without exception, but condensed into super-fast, apocalyptic summaries, for example, a book: just as we used to, seeing it coming, one or the other of us, this time he's the one who does the writing, revising it, I make lightning-quick corrections, he had other ideas as well for the future and on condition of course, all this we did with the same lightness and felicity, refusing to be dispirited by the brevity of the program, though I confess I was cranky, I was curt with people who'd have wasted my time, telling myself he'd chide me for this, but he didn't notice, so I did the right thing, there was a little of everything in these hours, this is what was so wonderful, all the genres but in a paroxysm, some grotesque as well but above all the wisdom of a kind of felicity of which I would never have believed us capable in peacetime. The dream as well in which we were on leave and which was called *A Leave*, we each lived-dreamed it in our own particular manner me from within, him more from without. I'm the one who told him the name of the dream, which had a name like the name of a city, and he as usual was half-skeptical half-mystical "as usual I am skeptimystic" my friend said, half thrilled that the thing was happening with a name and perhaps by the name, seeing where the name led, and that all this was possible, the worst having happened – which we never gave a name to, in our anxiety, but also because the thing hasn't any name. And we were thinking. As thinking beings, we were ultra-quick him especially. Millions of thoughts, torrents of them. "I wish I could believe you as we were wont to say," he thought and at the same time believing, sadly believing, sad-believing, because, as he thought, "this can only be happening if the worst has come to pass, but the worst is not this, if the worst seems to have happened it means the worst can't yet have happened" and I saw him thinking that, but from another side

So there may be leaves, I told myself and I tried to keep up with him despite the contradiction, which almost brought me to a halt, unthinkable, between the worst yet to come and the granting of leaves. And the proof is that what was granted on one side was withdrawn *on the other*, which was more or less what he felt, but one could still revel in the bliss of a moment. *There may be leaves!* I told myself. But this is your dream, he thought. Obviously, the condition of a leave is to be just a leave, I thought back. But on the other side, yours, it's you who gave me the idea of an incomprehensible but very real leave, I thought. We were thinking. To save time we read one another's thoughts at supernatural speed. What we had in common was this breakneck speed. We never left off thinking for even a fraction of a tenth of a second. Super-speed acquired by rubbing our two brains together beyond the speed of light for decades.

"Dream or no dream, it's" I thought. And he concurred. Not reality, reality realer than reality, and finally thought he "the Veridical." That's what we'll call it. I laughed. It was his *Ver* coming back. *Veridical*, I thought: a word I have never in my life to date employed.

Not in the least like a dream. "The Resurrection."

Resurrection is what one doesn't believe in. Believe in it and it doesn't exist, don't believe and it doesn't exist. A total absolute complete and limited resurrection. The resurrection's only hitch is its leave status. Far be it from me to complain. This is not your old-time resurrection. Not at all. This is the *resurrection of the present*. The friend who comes is not who he used to be, he's who he is now this very day such as he emerges from the wreck never before have I seen him in such a state, this gives rise to a frenzy of worry and chagrin but a fearful happiness both infinite and doomed shines out. Almost a day. A few hours, all of life's forces after death combined to substantiate a return to reality are enough to keep going for a few hours. Then this provisional life having *utterly* exhausted its store of energy grinds to a halt. The leave's last moments are dreadful. One feels the last drops of time oozing away and suddenly as if a call had sounded, nothing audible though, but a bell in a locatable part of the brain, one is warned that the time is up. Another half hour, now everything's jotted shorthand, broad strokes, so little time, there he goes, sentences shorter and shorter, one says: may I? the other: yes, then without warning he has to go, one has to let him go, so fast, no adieu.

So all is not lost I tell myself; therefore nothing being totally lost, nothing is lost. Something like the courage to be happy welled up in me and, though alive, the feeling of being brought back to life. Since leaves may be granted. All that is required is a revolution in our habits, the mind working on itself unceasingly so as to cast itself beyond itself, using its imagination to drag itself towards something it doesn't know how to get to, but this isn't so much to ask. I took the measure of the breadth and solidity of the anguish that had become my inner space of late by comparing it with the sudden feeling of emerging from a pulmonary cave-in and recovering the pleasure of breathing deeply which I didn't know I'd lost, sipping the air. All of a sudden I became again.

One discovers by breathing that one had stopped breathing. One only discovers one's stopped breathing when one takes the next breath.

Not that we were "liberated from the order of time" during the leave, quite the contrary. We were freed from the order of death, I tell myself, that's why time's order had never been so omnipresent and authoritative. So late do I discover the different "orders." For the first time I was discovering the complexities and the resources of "the order of death" of which hitherto I'd been unaware. Hence I had only just learned that after the knife falls, the great separator, after the last words of the Essay of Friendship ceased to resound there could be an other realm not totally closed-and-nothingness, a realm of retention not utterly cut off in a neverness, but with suspensions, remissions hesitations leaves, brief liftings of the latch. Now and then one could *re-establish the lines of communication that nourish friendship*. A sort of repairing of the line, such as I hadn't had the good fortune to work out with my father, for we hadn't had time to think together and to talk to each other at such length and so often on the telephone and maybe even never. That which affects us as being sick-to-death is to be localized in the complete and utter impotence to which I on my side saw myself yield like a pale imitation of the impotence-other on the side of my friend. Of late I hadn't even had enough strength to meditate on the evilness of his kidnapping, a weakness of my soul and my force of representation that I had all the difficulty in the world to resist, helpless as I was to reflect upon the ghastly mystery that had come over the ghost of my friend in the days preceding his leave: I noticed without comprehending it, without being able to analyze the dust-of-a-butterfly-wing substance of his presence, is it presence is it absence is absence not absence but feeble presence, a light –

too light – presence of my friend, and this was my fault, as if the ghost, who ought logically and naturally to be just the same whether he's gone off on a trip or on the Long Voyage, were of another species

As if the ghost of ordinary absence were nourished and kept alive by the certainty of return, hence by a mental or spiritual act due to belief. And as if, he having departed on what I believed to be the Long Voyage, the sort of nourishment and substantiality that safeguard the ghost's charm during his absence, were no longer dispensed, causing the ghost to waste away, the absent person's body to be dispersed, which I naturally thought was caused by the harshness of the kidnapping, by an inexorable debilitation of the person of his presence, a chastisement that brutally battered those of his nearest and dearest who pretended to act as if the irreversible had not occurred. But I was as wrong as can be. He hadn't wasted away I'd wasted him. Because I didn't *actively* believe he'd be back, without being cognizant of the danger I let in, I had starved the image, let it grow thin and pale for want of regular insufflations of patient waiting, of the familiar and gentle projection of return that safeguards our friends' thickness when they go off on a trip. Everything possible in the case of an absence (help, hope, waiting, patience, correspondence, calculation, the right to prayer and supplication) being null and void in the case of a Long Voyage, I'd let myself be stripped of my rights and prerogatives of invocation and be myself annulled.

The shock was the annulment of the annulment. I'd just awakened. And as if in the night I'd forgotten to believe or not believe, forgotten the wall, as in a dream I jumped up to answer the phone and where the wall was – no wall, I slipped through to the other side. And right away the leave began.

What the leave left me on deposit after the grace period expired: a crazy sad elation, as sad as it was exciting. A wretched happiness, yet another affect I've never suspected I could feel, a tearful happiness, lightened, raked by claws, to discover that death lets pass, that it may sheathe its claws, admit exceptions. As if one *could do* everything one imagines doing, all of us living dead dying life death and other beings subject to laws so harsh but open to interpretation, natural phenomena. An extra-mortal joy that doesn't take its eyes off death. No denials. I don't deny the sentence, its execution, its terrible consequences, the solitude, the weakening, the ruination of beauties the carnages of skies, global chlorosis, anxiety, that demolish us, the butchery of living moments, the pulling out by the roots of the hearts of things and beings. But that day it was clear to me we had found: the answer. This was the *Granting of Leave*. It will suffice.

The rest is patience, process, the search for new modes of existence in the double life.

Not that the death in my life became a matter of indifference to me; nor that the *insoluble difficulties* lost their importance and virulence, nor that I as if by magic suddenly found myself reconciled with destiny, nor that the ablation of my friend which began afresh each morning the minute I opened my eyes and thus the wound were stopped up, and not that it lost its ability to suppress the beauty of beautiful days to poison each meal and every page, but the synthesis of vivisection and nothingness that extended its infinite nothingness out from the window sill, from the edge of my lips, the abyss-nothingness that filled all the space in the world, but the hole turned into something. A horror but with pauses. It was no longer that nothing perpetual nothingness that compels us to renounce. I even had an inkling of a surprising advantage to the hard work in store: there could be no mourning, no growing accustomed to it. Above all, one could *hold onto* everything: the suffering to the quick and its whims, the sticky shadows, somber viscosity of the veil drawn taut around cities, everything could be borne, since legal outings of a few hours might take place, I told myself. Of course, I thought, no point pretending one wasn't dead. But on the other hand, rather than yield to the maneuvers of the conservation instinct, strategies that make us flee the pain within by hiding from ourselves within ourselves from whom we flee, its poppies, its hypnotic operations that the powerful currents of day-to-day life reinforce with a thousand vulgar, pressing duties which turn us from our hearts

do everything, I thought, on the contrary, whatever you can to resist the ingenious temptations of compromises, cling to the suffering, stir up the dread, for the monsters are also the benevolent guardians of the survivor's presence within me.

We were dying of death, one goes on dying for a very long time, but since we might see one another again,

life could ebb and flow, come back in go out again, I told myself, its warm flux irrigate all that was dead dying from the death of my friend, my animals, my trees my books my dreams all that was needed I told myself was to invent some superhuman strength, I prepared myself for huge unfamiliar kinds of anguish I know me I say I'm not good at waiting, doubt plants its hooks in me, but on the other hand I begin to believe again just as fast

"I can deal with this" I thought, "I'll start tomorrow." "Do what you need," he was thinking "Count on me," I thought back. Nothing being cut off. Besides I can count as well on the genius of my friend, I say, the sort of genius that has always meant going a leap beyond any other being in the world on the scent of the mind and spirit and especially going a leap beyond the place he himself imagined he could reach. What will make the wait so airless of course, I thought, is not to have any set date even a far-off one to hook the heart on and swing it over the abyss, it is at the mercy of all the horrors of waiting with which I am all too familiar (patience wearing thin, giving in to discouragement, the drying up of all the sublimating faculties, desertion of the passions, the abandonment of one's post, yielding to resentment). But underneath it all I tell myself the tiny glow-worm of the Leave event will be blinking. Up to me to surmount the trial, everything is dependent upon my will, impotent, tenacious, helpless, dogged, with a swollen sense of honor, I tell myself. I know me. Not that I'm the strongest as my friend used to claim, but I've always had the strength – weakness maybe – to believe that if "in the end we die, too fast," as he puts it, later on, as sequel, there's a chance that someone-I-don't-know-who – or I-don't-know-what – may come back. No keeping oneself from dying. Afterwards *nothing* stops one returning.

I then felt a joy not sharp deep and a little mad, the slight tipsiness of peace coming after a too-long pain when, having undergone the horrors of drowning, the worst of the human anguishes, the harrowing gulf coughs us back up again, air darts like an arrow into the lungs. So this life would not always be the glacial lifeless life into which I'd sunk alive lately, I tell myself. Once a year the colors will come back. Starting tomorrow, I'd thought. *Do what you need* he'd thought.

I'll do what it takes, helplessly. I say to myself, in an upsurge of sadness. My mission: submit to the absence without resisting without reckoning all the way to discouragement. Next dive into discouragement right to the pit of discouragement. After that there's a desert. Once in the desert, let yourself be vanquished.

Nothing more mysterious than to believe, unless it is to die. Believe, die, it clicks into place. Who knows why, there comes a moment, one believes, one dies. Suddenly one finds oneself on the other side without a trace of the way to the door on time's threshold no time no door. To believe resembles to die and vice versa to die is to arrest belief.

I jotted all this down as baggage for what might come. Life I knew would go back to death looking so much like it/him you couldn't tell them apart.

I wrote: "there are leaves" on a yellow post-it I stuck to the window over my desk. These post-its are tough, they look like nothing and go on for years.

The post-it will keep me company I thought, when I stop believing it will continue to believe.

I knew that right to the end of our days we'd be under the orders of death, from then on all I could hope for was loss after loss, one more dire than the next often it would be tough to breathe, I knew I'd want to die and that the order of the dead and the living would forbid this

but at least the horror of lugging lifeless life around a dead time was lightened by the thought of being able to taste *all life's riches* without exception, again, a few hours a year, I told myself, to be able to tell myself that in the end everything is returned to us, for as long it takes to recover the lost taste of writing, to smile at the sight of the voices coming to drink in the stairwell, overhear a scrap of meaningless yet archi-signed conversation, exchange a few words with a waitress in a café while hearing a hint of an accent chime in my friend's sentence, to be handed the world summed up in the dazzling brevity that illuminates him when, climbing two thousand meters above the planet in a little plane no bigger than a chair, life-size, the divine prop, one is granted permission to see everything one is from above.

How absolutely beautiful we are en masse and colored the bright colors we only see when we are neither inside nor outside, but pending. A-few-hours-a-year, I told myself again, for already I was counting on a small number of leaves, with the childish computations of the human being. Two years I tell myself without leave, for the moment is more than I can bear.

I took note of this program and its details, still basking in *the aura of the Leave's enigma*. I was in a rush to begin the work I knew awaited me, from now on I would have to believe, believe believe believe the unbelievable, saving up for the lean days when belief went dry.

In those lean days, going back to my store of notes, I'd know this had happened. I'd have a place to keep me safe from despair and forgetting, I'd cling to the raft of paper, keep my eye on the post-it. I covered dozens of pages. I was euphoric. "You for Rick?" my brother said. I managed to laugh. I'll be ready for famine. I worked like an ox.

In the hours following the leave I anoint Mummy with new sadness. Now her arms are so eaten up she modestly cloaks the dark mouths in gauze. She didn't let me do her arms. I'd kill her if I tried to have my way. I hallucinated, I picture infected sores too solemn to be unveiled in my presence. I take note that the malady speeds up its harvest. Evil feeds on evil. She's thriving. I no longer know long we'll hold on if the devouring takes Mummy's skin for springboard. But above all I caught myself thinking fearfully: Mummy won't come back. I was devastated by the idea that my mother would refuse to respond. Because she doesn't believe. Leaves are only granted those who *believed* in them before the passage. Or those who didn't believe but gave them some *thought*. Those who, not believing, would have liked to believe. My friend was never able to believe but he would have given a great deal to be able to believe had he been able to, he wouldn't have refused *to believe on my side*, even if on his side it had always been refused him to be able to believe there were leaves, it wasn't his fault he couldn't believe, he'd never had anything against the idea that I might be expecting some leaves, simply a sort of incredulity but admiring light generous which always encouraged me on my side to persist in my own line of thought even if he was watching me believe from his shore without even seeing me, like a blind Moses to whom someone paints the other shore: there is a mountain with a rosy top from whose summit you might catch a glimpse of the promised land. Whereas my mother, no. With me as with the butcher she adds up the bill. I decided I'd ask her if she'd come back.

I was on my knees in front of her. Her skin is worn so thin by the cortisone that she is covered with large violet splotches, bloody lakes formed by abrasion that leak at the slightest touch. She is wearing the openwork cotton cardigan my grandmother crocheted. She doesn't do it on purpose. She turns towards me. Her huge brown eyes are impatient at finding themselves snared in the old yellowing mesh of her face. In a hyperdream they would come and settle on my hands. I am a tattered old rag she says, you've said that before I say. *Ein Mangel*, you know that one? I know scarcity I say. Not *Mangel. Mangel.* To put the sheets through the wringer. If you put me through the *Mangel* nothing would come out the other side. Then the aura dissipates. This doesn't worry me. I've had my dream. My certificate of leave.

Naturally I'd only told my brother about the title and the "hat": "my friend J.D. on leave." Then, about the straw boater. That's all. Then the dry period began, this wasn't a problem. It was part of the plan. No visit. No leave. Then I have visions of dryness, sensations of dryness, dry throat, a cough and hundreds of those annoying dreams one knows are the usurpers: I dream abundantly of all those I do not love, above all the false friends. They press in. Homer knew this, at the head of the crowd shadows elbow aside those we love, our parents, to get themselves dreamed before the real ones. And all the people who attacked my father, and my friend. Which was, I grant you, one way of dreaming my way towards my own, but that I could have done without. When I have a worldwide feeling of dried-up wells I see the desert coming.

Then I decided to come back to my reservoir. If necessary one can catch one's breath on the lips of a dream but I've never felt the need to. In theory I don't use my old moments of happiness, I put my faith in the future. This will be the one exception I tell myself, I grant myself a special leave to make use of *A Special Leave*.

I don't find the *Leave*, I look for it, only a minute ago I was safe, I had my certificate of eternity, now the cavity is digging itself out in front of me, I search, the fires of terror roar at my window ledge, damnable chaos of books papers notebooks demented jungle of my toil I hook one last furious hope to your unleashing, perhaps you are the one who has hidden it, slipped it into one of your two hundred chinks of perfidiousness, already fear's suffering makes me sweat and quake, that the *Leave* not be in its place, already this is beyond imagining, it is blasphemy, it is most-unlikelihood, I had slipped it into a manuscript copy of *Fichus* my friend entrusted me with in August 2001, like the heart of gold in the chest of gold, that the dear sweet sheets not be where I myself so carefully laid them in the top left-hand drawer is a dart in my breast, an unbearable sign, a being-left-in-the-lurch without explanation, right away I shift into desperate search mode without missing a beat I search from the incongruous to the absurd to the impossible I turn up the whole field of paper, I go beyond sense, beyond the beyond of the reasonable, methodically and in vain.

At the end of the day I note some ashes: "for 6 hours looked in vain for the copy of *Fichus* with *A Leave* in it. Unfindable. Cannot conceive of greater pain. Incomprehensible. Hadn't made a copy, authentic madness. Infinite dolor. I am *fichue*, I am done for. 17-7-05"

Ashes of Event greatest catastrophe that could have occurred, collected in the Thériaque notebook.

Then the Leave *leaves. I search for it everywhere.* In the house. After all it wasn't a dream. I'm not crazy. I am crazy. I look all over for examples of comparable pain. Physical: hand torn off, eyes out. Metaphorical: soul transformed into a living torch. Literary aside from the disappearance of Albertine there are none. Spiritual: all the betrayals. But of them one dies fast.

I'm not able to reconstitute the dream. I hadn't wanted to appropriate it or reread it or learn it by heart, in order – what a thought – for it not to lose its virginity, the freshness of the just-barely-glimpsed, for the day when I would give myself the miracle again. I remember the hat. Suddenly I recognize that hat. It's the hat in Benjamin's "*fichu* dream." I reread *Fichus*, the straw hat is on page 38, an "old straw hat" a "panama" says my friend that Benjamin inherited from his father and which had, in his dream, a big crack in the top, with "a trace of red" on the edge, says my friend, at least the hat is not lost I tell myself, it was handed down from Benjamin's father to Benjamin's dream, which handed it on to my friend, from whom I have inherited it, which I *found* on my desk in the very place I can no longer put my hands on the Mystical sheet of paper, the Leave treatise, instead of a peace treaty with the powers of death I've come up with this hat I couldn't put down, which dogged me everywhere, which I held out to my daughter but just for a second, which I took back, which I held out to my friend who held it defenselessly, without refusing, without taking offense, without our having at any moment understood, suspected, received the intimation, which this hat is, has always been the container of, the sign the message of, that I have just, in my useless attempt to reconstitute the dream, perceived. "It's the *fichu* hat" I cried in a transport of panic and terror, having suddenly realized that during this whole time of ecstasy I hadn't for an instant been separated from this token of death which I had absent-mindedly held out to my daughter, that my friend had then held for me, in the middle of our bliss we'd had our hands on the calamity, I thought this hat was silly, all the same in my mind it was the very picture of the hats my young father affected. And as I experienced the sad happiness of the revelation which sheds light on the hat I groan with terror at discovering its tragic origin and, as I groan with terror because I have just spotted the worm, I feel a bizarre joy at having held this funereal and magic hat in my hands but torn by the thought that I no longer have any part of the Leave, as with paradise only the gate remains, only the hat, both an essential element of the dream and prophetic warning. As if we entered into happiness on condition of calamity. I'd snatched up the hat when the phone rang, and right to the very last ring it stayed with us. I was supposed to keep it, it seemed to me, and give it back to somebody.

What I took for a *hat* – a *chapeau* – I realize, is an honest and truly homemade bomb: all the catastrophes and all the dead are housed in it, the fate of me and mine, the threats, the maladies, the boil that devours my mother's skin – her *peau* – and even a burning reminder of the death of my beloved cat – my *chat* – of which I never spoke to anyone save to my love and save to my friend who was fond of it and who could understand that my cat was the steadiest and purest of creatures in love that I have ever, in this world, caressed. Now the hat – the *chat/peau* – bobs in my memory as on Lethe an urn.

The pain of having lost the dream of the Leave, therefore the Leave, is so wrenching that it almost amounts to reliving the pain of losing my friend, I believed I'd never again feel this frenzy, therefore one may suffer from the same death twice, I didn't know. When I turn the house upside down it's not even to locate it, something I no longer believe in, it's out of frenzy.

I didn't make a copy. Only myself to blame. I blame everyone in sight. Someone stole it. It's been stolen. I blame myself. I attempt a summary. Not much of a trace. I know that only the whole dream will cure me. Nothing will give it back. There is only one original.

What I'd saved: lost. Worse: *I lost it.* Can't even tell myself that I sort of lost it that lost I keep it still. I lost the saved.

I've lost. I'm lost.

This is a pain one dies of or kills. Kill it and one kills oneself.

Splashes of bloody skin all over my notebooks.

I haven't *forgotten* a dream, as it is written happens in the realm of dreams. One forgets a dream, then one forgets one has forgotten, nothing dies of this.

I've lost *The Dream.*

I cannot tell a soul. I will not enter alive into the beyond. I search for an explanation. To the labyrinth I descend with the *chapeau*. Maleficent remains but remains, therefore blessed. If I could ask my friend. No one else. He and only he knows the extraordinary value of what is lost, greater by far than the value of what one keeps. Suddenly I'm only this torch consuming itself. What to do? I had the papers, I took them from myself, I threw them in the Trash, I threw out my own being, I had the memory of the future at the window I broke me, I tore up the secret into a thousand pieces, I tweezed the sublime out of me, I had god I squashed him with a hat,

this is not the first time I take myself to the labyrinth but this is the first time I go down into the labyrinth. I went right by the very trash bin of my being, how can you do away with your own eyes, I did it, who knows how

I was on top of the world I'm down in the dumps, some instinct wants me out. "Instinct?" What kind of word is that? I'm scared of this "instinct" whose beast of burden I've become. It's strange to want who knows what, to obey who knows what, and it's black as pitch in here. *Sortir. Sort tire. Sors, tire.* Leave. Fate tugs. Leave, pull out. I forget. Do what? I remind myself: find my cat, get myself unstuck from this hat.

Heart and soul I summon my cat, body no, telephone no, trumpet no, blare no. I recall my friend saying that there is one possibility, now no more possibility, into the bin. I've got you in the waste paper bin I say, if only the letters told the truth but bin is just a metaphor. Questions stop me in the tunnel – What is your cat like? – Good-looking, slim, small, tigerish grey. – Where's your bag? – Your turn now? – What? Where? – In the bag, the charred scarf of – Bumbling to

The station, that's where everything becomes impossible. Stay in the middle and the tunnel will take us all the way to ramallah providing we are prepared to spend the night. Straight ahead. Otherwise there's spain, or london even, half an hour. I give up. To get to the station you must cut through the swimming pool, frightening because it's empty and you see its big fat tongue lolling out, no water, no edge, friends and family all on the other side, I force myself to detour round. All this would like to keep me at arm's length, separate me. It's because of the disappearance of the alliance, hence of the light that I've kidnapped myself. Almost train time. I haven't got the cat. I shout to my daughter to shepherd the family onto the platform and I go after our cat. No sign of it like the Messiah. A tiny little cat comes up to me, ugly, palm-sized, more like a monkey with a purple back, hairless, bewigged, mewling to be adopted. I am touched, then I say no. Poor thing clings to me, follows me everywhere, desperately I look for ours along with this poor monkey, touching ugly bald with its wig at my heels. I don't chase it away.

Here it is, shouts my daughter, we found it! My family holds it up from afar I make out the white bag we packed it in for the trip. Surely my cat in that shawl-thing, I take their word for the thing I don't see. "Run! Run!" I say. To whom? The only thing in sight is the violet cat. We run. Why do I dive down under the earth to get to the other side? Alas, when I come up I am completely elsewhere, nowhere, more lost than ever, I remember nothing – no one – I sit down on the earth and I fall asleep. And then my daughter knocks me over. A sentence sobs: don't you see it's an effigy? Who? who? I shout. Who? I think. Since they are getting scared, I call out: who? how? As if that might be a dead body. – A degraded effigy of *le jeune singe juif*, the young Jewish monkey-saint don't you see? And then a blinding light, how cruel the repetition! I felt everything, I understood nothing, what was the good of the *Befindlichkeit*, this foundling of a monkey that clung to me, desiring only to grant my every wish, how polite how patient how bald how confident how full of humor, he asked nothing better, all it took was a wig and once again I got everything wrong, I have a fork in my heart, endless loss, I tell myself (and there's not even any I to lay me down to sleep or to bereft me) one wakes too late

What have I done to myself? Auto-immunity theme? The theme my friend was tracking down. Theme of the forbidden? I believed that mortals were allowed to enjoy some godlike privileges and for that I was punished? Or I wanted to short-cut suffering with this magic pass-key and at the same time I wanted just the opposite, I wanted, the same person wanted to revive suffering, keep it alive, keep loss simmering?

So what lay in wait for me was not the Leave. It was the eternal recommencement of the loss. There was something pernicious right to the words with which I deluded myself, I hadn't caught the hint of crime in the word. *Leave: per-mission* in French; leave whose disastrous author I was, perhaps I was the plaything of the antique orphic anguish perhaps I'd tried to go in two different directions with a single force, I wanted to go on living on the hypothesis of leaves being granted but perhaps inside me *the other side*, my friend's, truth to tell, had blazed itself a voice to which I'd never on my own have considered yielding, but which spoke to me with an authority I couldn't not wish to yield to, supposing it was my friend's, providing I myself remain unaware of this. If this analysis is correct, I tell myself, that would explain how, having descended with my friend into the labyrinth, I can only ever find myself lost, that I never find save to lose, according to a law not my own but which, in my friend's tragic logic, with which I am so familiar, creates a synonymy between finding and losing. So in order to remain faithful to him, despite myself (to remain on the side of his inability to believe in the granting of leaves) I had simultaneously to be unfaithful (despite myself whole-heartedly resist his conviction by taking a firm stand on the side of leaves) while inside my unfaithfulness I would remain faithful to him against him in spite of him by being unfaithful with a superior brand of faithfulness (stick to my guns by *giving* him the benefit of doubt so as to overcome his disbelief for his sake, despite the anxiety that my refusal to rally his cause caused me). I don't know where this labyrinth is leading me, here I am losing again, it's all the same to me and I'm exhausted.

July 24. *A Leave* came back. Gone for good for a week, I barred it, I lost my friend's Leave. I wept over it. It has *come back*.

I didn't *find* it, I noted.

I don't stop 1) losing 2) searching 3) searching without finding.

Sometimes the lost find their own way back. I don't find them.

I lost hope. I am in command of nothing.

– Will you come back? I ask my mother. – Where? – Here I say. I point to the study. – To the house. – I haven't gone anywhere yet, she says. I'm not a spirit to come knocking she says. At home we say *Vutsch is Vutsch. Hin ist Hin.*

I ask her to spell *Vutsch* for me. – *Vutsch* I say, is done for? – Done for, *fichu*, says my mother. I'm not bothered about anything says my mother, except my white saucers you must be taking for your cats. I would like them to come back. You don't stop taking my saucers. Someone is filching my saucers. I've lost another one. It doesn't stop.

Translator's Notes

I am often asked how closely I work with Hélène Cixous when I am translating one of her books.

As a rule, I complete my translation – wearing away little by little at the difficult points – before showing it to Hélène Cixous. Eventually – original flagged with post-its, penciled notes and questions to myself or to her, translated text blinking with highlighted words, sentences, paragraphs – I print off a copy and send it to her, and we make a date to talk about it: about my queries, and whatever she spots in her own reading of the translation: difficulties I have overlooked, as well as my misinterpretations and approximations. I must, however, emphasize how very busy she is; she has never pretended to have time to examine a translation sentence by sentence.

So I am the only person who reads and rereads the translation, and therefore the sole responsible for the errors and omissions, which undoubtedly occur, as I have, ruefully, had occasion to notice. Furthermore, however close I wish to remain to the original – and I do – I am of necessity constantly interpreting. For instance, *Hyperrêve* (p. 42) has a sentence: "*Pendant ce temps-là nous vivons.*" "During this time we live, we are living, we go on living?" I eliminate the last possibility, because "*nous continuons à vivre*" is thematized elsewhere in the text, but how to choose between the first two tenses? Do I prefer the rhythm of one or the other? If I write "we are living," whose rhythm I prefer in that sentence, it might be translated back into French here as "*nous sommes vivants*" ("we are alive"), which is not what Cixous has written. In this case, therefore, I translate *nous vivons* as " we live" (p. 27).

The choice, however, may seem – even to me – at times arbitrary, resulting as it does from a myriad of infinitesimal, perhaps partly intuitive, but important adjustments of tone, sentence rhythm, assonance and alliteration, always – it goes without saying – seeking to render as closely as possible *all* the language aspects of a text, of which dictionary meaning is just one. "Literal" is a word both Cixous and Derrida play on, defining it as "to the letter," which they mean *literally*. Cixous's choice of diction, I am aware, may be dictated as much by the sounds of a word as by what we are used to call its meaning.

Of course, I do not underestimate the difficulties that arise from the polysemy, synonymy, homonymy and homophony that are characteristic of Cixous's writing, and which are one element of her voice, as are her abrupt shifts of style, from analysis to narrative to dialogue, from the familiar to the philosophical. Characters' voices are at times mingled to the point where it may be difficult to know where one stops and another begins, and she plays fruitfully with such ambiguities. Demarcations between direct and indirect speech may be left deliberately vague. All these elements, and many more (the question of gender, the differences and difficulties of translating pronouns, the implications of syntax and tense differences between French and English) are essential to Cixous's – or the book's – desire to capture thought, feeling and experience, with their complexities and ambiguities, and to land them still shimmering with life on the pages of the book.

Others, including Cixous's friend Jacques Derrida, have written about these aspects of her writing. What I wish to say is that as a translator I have thought it important to be as attentive to the poetic force of concision, collision, fragmentation, the headlong rush of thoughts, the hesitations, confusions of characters and voices and the sounds of words and voices on the page as to their etymologies and dictionary meanings. Translating one of Hélène Cixous's texts presents many – most – of the challenges of translating poetry.

I have not wished to include footnote numbers within the body of the text. Instead, I have juxtaposed French with English within the text, when I felt it would illuminate a particular difficulty or play on words, particularly for readers with a reading knowledge of both languages. The notes below are intended to signal a few allusions which may be less familiar to English readers than they are to the French, and some plays on words which proved particularly resistant to translation.

AUTHOR'S FOREWORD

The Author's Foreword is a "Prière d'insérer" or loose sheet of paper containing a text by the author that serves as publicity material. These are increasingly rare in French publishing.

you are time, killing time (p. vii): the French says *tu es le temps*, which means "you are time"; however, *tu es le temps* sounds like *tuer le temps*, "killing/to kill time." The text plays on this homophony.

I anoint my old helmet-maker *ma vieille beaulmière* (p. x): *la (belle) beaulmiére* is a figure from François Villon's *Testament*.

lostness (p. 7): Cixous invents a word here: *perdution*, in which one hears *perdu*, "lost," and "perdition."

cadaverized jellyfish, a medusa (p. 11): *petite méduse cadavérisée* in French. The word for "jellyfish" in French is *méduse*.

BENJAMIN'S BED

In French the title is "Le Sommier de Benjamin" (and not "Le Lit de Benjamin"). The object is a *sommier métallique*: that is, a metal bedframe, presumably on legs, with stretched wire slats or (flat) springs. In North America such an object is often known as "bedspring(s)," a translation which resonated with the picaresque side of the bed's adventures in the life of the narrator. "Bedstead" was another possibility, even if such an old and old-fashioned word was ill adapted to an object which once purportedly belonged to the author of "The Work of Art in the Age of Mechanical Reproduction." So, after consulting informants on both sides of the Atlantic, and with some regret, "bed" was adopted, occasionally modified for contextual reasons to "bedframe."

A further complication is that the word *sommier* occurs frequently in the original French text, in wordplays with *un somme* (from Latin *somnus, sleep*): a "nap" or "snooze." It also occurs once in *bête de somme*, beast of burden, and several times as *une somme* in the sense of "sum." In these places, I have often resorted to using the French words *sommier . . . somme* in conjunction with their English translations.

Fichus (p. 65): *Fichus* is the title of the speech Derrida delivered on September 22, 2001 in Frankfurt on the occasion of being awarded the Adorno Prize. The title comes from a letter Walter Benjamin wrote on October 12, 1939 to Gretel Adorno about a dream in which he says to himself, in French: "*Il s'agissait de changer en fichu une poésie*" ("It was about turning a poem into a scarf"). In French a *fichu* (pl. *fichus*) is a small, triangular shawl or scarf a woman throws over her head or shoulders. However, familiarly, the word stands in for the less polite *foutre*, and means "rotten, awful"; hence the turn of phrase *être fichu*: "to be done for." The English translation of Derrida's speech *Fichus* can be found in his collection *Paper Machine* (Stanford University Press, 2005).

Albertine (p. 65) is a central character in Marcel Proust's *À la recherche du temps perdu*; she is the prisoner of the volume called *La Prisonnière*.

there's an *auteur*, an *ôteur*, a plotter and deleter (p. 67): a neologism, *ôteur* plays on the sounds and meaning of the verb *ôter* (to remove) and the noun *auteur* (author).

right away I find the Bed (p. 69): letter 267 in *The Correspondence of Walter Benjamin* (Chicago: University of Chicago Press, 1994), p. 510.

the blue-trimmed sail (p. 72): in French *la voile*, sail; perhaps one should also hear *le voile*, veil. In Benjamin's letter to Gretel Adorno of October 12, 1939 as translated in *The Correspondence of Walter Benjamin* (see previous note), Benjamin writes: "Appended to this part of the letter was a small sail with a blue border, and the sail was billowing as if filled by the wind." However, the same letter, as reproduced in *Gretel Adorno and Walter Benjamin: Correspondence 1930–1940* (Cambridge: Polity Press, 2008), speaks of "a small piece of fabric with a blue border." The original letter, written in

French to facilitate the work of censors (during WB's internment in the Nevers "Centre des travailleurs volontaires"), says "*la voile*"; however, Benjamin asks his correspondent to forgive him any errors in this letter written in the hubbub of the camp (*Walter Benjamin: Gesammelte Briefe, Band VI, 1938–1940*, Frankfurt: Suhrkamp, 2000).

the *Livre de la Thériaque* (p. 103) is an Arab manuscript held in the French National Library. A medical treatise, it contains antidotes to stings, bites and poisons of all sorts.

this being-ableness, this reason-ableness (p. 111): French *ce pourrement, cettepourraison* – a play on *pouvoir* (to be able) and *raison* (reason).

***The last word* (p. 125):** *Le fin mot – fin* means "end" in French and *mot* means "word," but the idiomatic expression *le fin mot* means a word or phrase that acts as the key to an enigma.

the quartered hour (p. 130): in French the daughter explains that there is a bus "*tous les quarts d'heure*"; growing impatient, the mother, asks: "*Où est l'écart d'heure?*" In reporting this conversation, the narrator uses *écart*, a word whose many connotations in Cixous's writing unfortunately get lost in translation. I have chosen to use "quartered" (*écartelé*).

A LEAVE

It was his *Ver* coming back (p. 144): *Un ver à soie* ("A Silkworm") is the title of one of Derrida's texts.

I was euphoric. "You for Rick?" (p. 152): The French says "*J'étais dans l'euphorie*" ("I was in euphoria"), to which the brother, playing on the sounds of *euphorie*, jokingly or mockingly, playing on the sounds of *euphorie*, replies "*Tu es dans l'oeuf au riz?*" ("You are in the egg with the rice?")

A degraded effigy of *le jeune singe juif*, the young Jewish monkey-saint (p. 159): *Saint juif*, literally "Jewish saint," sounds like *singe juif*, or "Jewish monkey." *Portrait de Jacques Derrida en Jeune Saint Juif (Portrait of Jacques Derrida as a Young Jewish Saint)* is the title of a book by Hélène Cixous. The book title plays on this homophony.